GERMAN ILLUMINATION

GERMAN ILLUMINATION

BY

ADOLPH GOLDSCHMIDT

Professor in the University of Berlin

VOLUME I

CAROLINGIAN PERIOD

Reprinted by

HACKER ART BOOKS

NEW YORK

1970

First Published in 1928

by Pantheon—Casa Editrice—Florence

Reprinted 1970

by HACKER ART BOOKS—New York

Library of Congress Catalog Card Number 72-78259

CONTENTS

PREFACE

NO SELECTION of examples of mediaeval book decoration and miniature painting, and no short account of the development of these arts will be likely to please all tastes or satisfy all requirements. While the expert prefers to see new and rare things calculated to widen his knowledge, the less informed requires examples of a definite and distinct style put clearly before his eyes. However, such have most likely already been reproduced elsewhere. An attempt therefore is made in the following plates to combine less familiar illustrations, not yet reproduced, with classic examples. The author has wished above all to collect several works of each school, so that the student may gain a clear idea of the various styles, rather than pass in review a number of isolated reproductions. As a result of this method the illustrations are necessarily restricted to manuscripts from the most important centers. Works of the smaller scriptoria, scattered all over Germany, are omitted.

The choice of a title was not an easy matter. The catchwords «Carolingian» and «Ottonian» do not always satisfactorily express the periods to which these miniatures belong. On the contrary, stylistic dividing lines could more easily be drawn about 950 and 1050: but as the foundations of the two styles were laid during the reigns of the Carolingian rulers and the Ottos, or Saxon emperors, the terms are partially justified. The beginnings of the periods are strictly marked respectively by the work of Charlemagne at the end of the eighth century, and the revival of learning in the monasteries toward the close of the reign of Otto I. At the end the line of demarcation cannot be so strictly drawn, as the influence of certain schools continues for many decades. Indeed, neither can the treatment of some of the miniatures executed in the beginning of the eleventh century easily be separated from certain Carolingian works, nor the Ottonian manner from the early Romanesque style of the second half of the eleventh century. Therefore, the division of this work into volumes must not be taken too strictly.

As the present volume deals only with German illumination, many manuscripts of French origin important from an artistic standpoint, were necessarily omitted; however, these have already been published by Boinet and the Comte de Bastard. On the other hand, two of the oldest and most important groups could be claimed for Germany.

For detailed information about the origin, date, contents and other particulars of the various manuscripts, the reader is referred to the tables, in order to avoid breaking the continuity of the text. As the originals could not be reconsulted in every case, the tables are not uniformly complete, and it was sometimes necessary to omit indication of the colours. For their elaboration and for other remarks, the author is particularly indebted to Dr. Albert Boeckler, who often could complete his notes. In the preparation of the plates, in addition to the photographs acquired for this book, he was able to avail himself of the material collected by Professor Arthur Haseloff, Dr. Wilhelm Köhler, Dr. Albert Boeckler, and the late Dr. Adolf Merton, and takes pleasure in expressing his heartfelt gratitude to all these scholars.

For the comprehensive revision of the English translation he is greatly indebted to Professor A. Kingsley Porter and to Mr. Walter M. Whitehill of Harvard College.

LIST OF PLATES

82 CASSEL, Landesbibliothek. Cod. theol. fol. 60. See plate 81. A. *Crucifixion with St. Mary and St. John, Terra, Sol and Luna.* B. *The women at the Tomb and the Harrowing of Hell.*

83 A. BERLIN, Staatsbibliothek. Cod. theol. lat. quart. 5. Gospels from St. Mauritius in Magdeburg. *The Evangelist Matthew.*
    B. MUNICH, Staatsbibliothek. Cod. lat. 10077 (Cim. 143). Sacramentary from the Cathedral treasury of Verdun. *Fragmentary representation of Pentecost.*

84 LEIPZIG, Stadtbibliothek. Cod. CXC. Two separate leaves of a Sacramentary stitched into Gospel manuscript of Reichenau. A. *Crucifix between Virgin and St. John.* B. *St. Gregory.*

85 WOLFENBÜTTEL, Landesbibliothek. 16. 1. Aug. fol. Heinemann 2187. Gospels. *Annunciation to the Shepherds.*

86 WOLFENBÜTTEL, Landesbibliothek. 16. 1. Aug. fol. Heinemann 2187. See plate 85. *Adoration of the Magi.*

87 ZÜRICH, Stadtbibliothek. Ms. C. 80. Dialectic and Rhetoric of Albinus. *Maiestas Domini.*

88 DÜSSELDORF, Landesbibliothek. A. 44. Epistles of St. Paul. *St. Paul.*

BIBLIOGRAPHY WITH ABBREVIATIONS

ADA-Hs. ⁄ *Die Trierer Ada Handschrift.* Bearb. u. hrsg. v. Menzel, Corssen, Janitschek, Schnütgen u. Hettner — Publikationen der Gesellschaft für Rhein. Gesch. Kunde, VI, Leipzig, 1899.

ARNETH ⁄ JOSEPH RITTER V. ARNETH, *Über das Evangeliar Karls des Grossen in der K. K. Schatzkammer,* Wien, 1864. With colour plates — Denkschriften der Wiener Akad. d. Wissensch., Phil.-Hist. Kl., XIII, S. 85 ff.

BANGE, *Malerschule* ⁄ E. F. BANGE, *Eine Bayerische Malerschule des XI. u. XII. Jhrhs.* München, Hugo Schmidt, 1923.

BASTARD ⁄ AUGUSTE COMTE DE BASTARD, *Peintures et ornements de manuscrits.* Paris, 1835 ff.

BEISSEL, *Evang. Bch.* ⁄ BEISSEL, STEPHAN, S. J., *Geschichte der Evangelienbücher in der ersten Hälfte des Mittelalters* — Stimmen aus Maria Laach. Erg. Bd. XXIII, Freiburg, 1906.

BEISSEL, *Vat. Min.* ⁄ STEPHAN BEISSEL, S. J., *Vatikanische Miniaturen* — Quellen zur Gesch. der Buchmalerei, Freiburg, 1893.

BERNATH ⁄ M. BERNATH, *Malerei des Mittelalters.* Leipzig 1916, — Woltmann u. Woermann, Geschichte der Malerei, I.

BETHE ⁄ ERICH BETHE, *Terentius, Codex Ambrosianus H. 75 inf.* — Codices graeci et latini photographice depicti duce scatone de Vries. Tom. VIII, Leyden, Sijthoff, 1903.

BOINET ⁄ AMADÉE BOINET, *La Miniature Carolingienne,* Paris, 1913.

BRAUN ⁄ EDMUND BRAUN, *Beiträge zur Geschichte der Trierer Buchmalerei im frühen Mittelalter* — Westdeutsche Zeitschrift für Geschichte u. Kunst. Erg. Heft IX (1895).

CHROUST ⁄ ANTON CHROUST, *Monumenta Palaeographica.* — Denkmäler der Schreib-kunst des Mittelalters. Ser. I. 1902-06; Ser. II. 1911-17. München, Bruckmann.

CLEMEN, *Fulda* ⁄ PAUL CLEMEN, *Studien zur Geschichte der karolingischen Kunst, I: Die Schreibschule von Fulda* — Repertorium für Kunstwissenschaft XIII, 1890.

DOERING u. VOSS ⁄ O. DOERING u. G. VOSS, *Meisterwerke der Kunst in Sachsen u. Thüringen.* Magdeburg, E. Baensch jun. 1905.

EHL ⁄ HEINRICH EHL, *Die Kölner ottonische Buchmalerei* — Forschungen zur Kunstge-schichte Westeuropas, hrsg. v. Eugen Lüthgen, Bd. VI. Bonn u. Leipzig, 1922.

GOLDSCHMIDT ⸗ ADOLPH GOLDSCHMIDT, *Die Elfenbein⸗Skulpturen aus der Zeit der karolingischen u. sächsischen Kaiser.* Bd. I u. II, Berlin, Bruno Cassirer, 1914 u. 1918.

HASELOFF, *Egb. Psalter* ⸗ HEINRICH VOLBERT SAUERLAND U. ARTHUR HASE⸗ LOFF, *Der Psalter Erzbischof Egberts v. Trier* — Festschrift der Gesellschaft für nützliche Forschungen, Trier, 1901.

HASELOFF, *Malerschule* ⸗ ARTHUR HASELOFF, *Eine thüringisch⸗sächsische Malerschule des 13. Jahrhs.,* Strassburg, Heitz, 1897.

HERBERT ⸗ J. A. HERBERT, *Illuminated Manuscripts,* London, 1911.

HERMANN ⸗ HERM. JUL. HERMANN, *Die früh⸗mittelalterlichen Handschriften des Abend⸗ landes* — Beschreibendes Verzeichnis der illuminierten Hss. in Oesterreich. N. F. I. (Wien, Nat. Bibl.), Leipzig, 1923.

KÖHLER, *Adagruppe* ⸗ WILH. KÖHLER, *Die Tradition der Adagruppe und die Anfänge des ottonischen Stils in der Buchmalerei* — Festschrift zum 60. Geburtstag v. Paul Clemen, S. 255, Düsseldorf, Schwann, 1926.

KUGLER ⸗ FRANZ KUGLER, *Kleine Schriften u. Studien zur Kunstgeschichte,* Stuttg. 1853/54.

LANDSBERGER ⸗ ARTHUR LANDSBERGER, *Der St. Galler Folchard⸗Psalter. Eine Initialstudie.* St. Gallen, 1912.

MERTON ⸗ ADOLF MERTON, *Die Buchmalerei in St. Gallen vom 9. bis zum II. Jahrh.* Leipzig, Hiersemann, 1912.

MICHEL ⸗ ANDRÉ MICHEL, *Histoire de l'Art,* I, 2, Paris, 1905.

SCHLOSSER ⸗ JULIUS V. SCHLOSSER, *Eine Fuldaer Min.⸗Hs. der K. K. Hofbibl.* — Jahrbuch der Kunsthist. Sammlgn. d. Allerhöchsten Kaiserhauses, XIII (1892), S. 1 ff.

SCHMIDT ⸗ ADOLF SCHMIDT, *Die Miniaturen des Gero⸗Codex,* Leipzig, Hiersemann, 1924.

STETTINER ⸗ RICH. STETTINER, *Die illustrierten Prudentius⸗Handschriften* (Strassburger Dissert. 1895). Berlin, Grote, 1905.

STRZYGOWSKI ⸗ JOSEF STRZYGOWSKI, *Das Etschmiadzin⸗Evangeliar* — Byzantinische Denkmäler, I, Wien, 1891.

SWARZENSKI, I ⸗ GEORG SWARZENSKI, *Die Regensburger Buchmalerei des 10.⸗11. Jh.* — Denkmäler der süddeutschen Malerei d. frühen Mittelalters, I, Leipzig, 1901.

SWARZENSKI, II ⸌ GEORG SWARZENSKI, *Die Salzburger Malerei von den ersten An⸌fängen bis zur Blütezeit des romanischen Stiles* — Denkmäler der süddeutschen Malerei d. frühen Mittelalters, II, Leipzig, 1914.

SWARZENSKI, *Reims* ⸌ GEORG SWARZENSKI, *Die karolingische Malerei und Plastik in Reims* — Jahrbuch d. Kgl. Preuss. Kunstslg., XXIII (1902), S. 81.

WARNER ⸌ GEORGE F. WARNER, *Illuminated Manuscripts of the British Museum*, London, 1903.

WEBER ⸌ LOUIS WEBER, *Einbanddecken, Elfenbeintafeln, Miniaturen, Schriftproben aus Metzer liturg. Handschriften*, Metz u. Frankfurt a. M., 1912.

ZIMMERMANN ⸌ E. HEINRICH ZIMMERMANN, *Die Fuldaer Buchmalerei in karolingischer u. ottonischer Zeit* — Kunstgeschichtliches Jahrbuch der K. K. Zentralkommission zur Erhaltung u. Erforschung der Kunst⸌ u. historischen Denkmale, IV (1910), S. 1.

ZIMMERMANN ⸌ E. HEINRICH ZIMMERMANN, *Vorkarolingische Miniaturen* — Denkmä⸌ler deutscher Kunst, III. Sektion, 1. Abt., Berlin, 1916. Deutscher Verein für Kunst⸌wissenschaft.

THE TEXT

ONE of the most important heritages transmitted by the later antique civilization, perhaps the most important, was the book. Not only did it constitute the mainstay of the Christian mission, not only was it instrumental in handing down to the Middle Ages the science and literature of the classical past, but also through its decorations it facilitated the transmission of the style of antique painting, although not always in its purest form. In the north, the book was the starting point for the pictorial representation of the visible world, of human and divine events, and until the beginning of the Gothic period, retained its sway in the domain of artistic creation, including plastic art. As no other art in its present state exhibits a wealth and continuity equal to that of book-decoration, the book remains the most solid basis for the criticism of mediaeval artistic expression and for the appraisement of its relations to both nature and decorative skill. There is no doubt that, compared with illumination, monumental art and mural painting, as developed on the walls of churches and palaces, may be considered as the more important, and as requiring greater artistic power. As monumental painting was constantly before the eyes of the bulk of the people, it was instrumental in impressing upon the mind of the masses the conception of the history of the Passion, of Biblical narratives, of theological phantasies and of dogmatic allegories. The decorated book, at least during the first centuries of our era, was exclusively in the hands of the clergy and the inmates of monasteries, but as these were the bearers of tradition it was precisely the book which fostered this tradition. The book furnished the subject matter from which not only generations of illustrators but also monumental painters drew their inspiration.

In its essence, the book is a product of the fourth century, of the time when the codex generally began to take the place of the scroll. The libraries of that time demanded a transcription into stitched books of the literature handed down in the shape of scrolls, and the period in which this process took place is in some respects of the greatest importance. The literary taste of the people of that time was the decisive circumstance in the handing down to posterity of older works. Whatever was considered valuable in those days was transcribed and thus saved for future copies, while all the literature left only in scrolls gradually, for the most part, perished, unless some amateur of a later age occasionally brought it to light again. It was therefore the literary taste of the fourth and fifth centuries that determined the preservation of classical tradition.

When the bearers of Christianity, coming from the South, crossed the Alps or on their way from the Syrian and African coasts landed on the Western shores of Europe, or when the Northern missionaries returned home from their travels, books constituted the chief treasure which they carried with them. In the book they found not only instruction and guidance for divine service, the history of the Passion and its interpretation by the Fathers of the Church, but also much medical and astronomical instruction.

All the information which, through many small and separate channels, had flowed among the new nations who were just entering upon the stage of the world's history, was for the first time systematically and with uniform care collected under Charlemagne. At his court the Emperor gathered prominent men from all the geographical and linguistic regions of his own and the neigh- bouring kingdoms, and entrusted to them the task of establishing centres for the promotion of education and the collection of literature. The best texts of religious and scientific works were procured, frequently copied and widely diffused.

Some of these books contained not only texts but also illustrations. They need not even have been numerous in order to establish the connection between the old and the new art of illumination. People often fail to form a right idea of the widespread influence which a single codex could exercise. One illumi- nated manuscript, introduced in the scriptorium of some monastery, may for generations have fecundated the style of illumination in that monastery. The flame once kindled continued to burn. It was not always a question of mere copying, for the gifted artist soon began to vary and combine and, availing himself of his model but relying on his own imagination, to reproduce simi- lar scenes after the style of his predecessor. The technical execution underwent a change, the colours were altered. In view of the fragmentary nature of the

2

evidence in our possession, a strict affiliation can of course be proved only in rare cases, but we are justified in our assumption that even in the Carolingian age one manuscript must often have become the starting point of far-reaching artistic traditions.

For figure drawing north of the Alps, Southern England and the Frankish Kingdom were the decisive centers. From these countries constant influence upon German soil took place, while the direct importation from the South into German monasteries must have been of a merely sporadic nature.

There are three different ways of obtaining a comprehensive survey of German illumination which is more than a casual listing of works. We can either collect into groups all the manuscripts of similar style, or, proceeding from the place where the works happen to be preserved at present, make a sort of inventory of the most important manuscripts found in various libraries and museums, or finally, we can occupy ourselves with the old monasteries and, calling to our aid palaeography and history, endeavour to ascertain which of the manuscripts were executed in their scriptoria and thus make an historical and geographical classification. The second way is the more external and unscientific, although it is to be recommended when it is simply a question of gaining a provisional acquaintance with the entire material. If we wish, however, to arrive at an historical appreciation, we shall have to adopt both the first and third ways. Both do not lead us to the same result, but they complement and correct each other, thus helping us to the clearest possible perception of realities.

In this way it becomes evident that in the various scriptoria, particularly in the more important ones, there was more than one style in vogue. Not only were the existing stocks of manuscripts heterogeneous in character, for new works constantly came into the libraries both as gifts and as acquisitions, but even those which were being produced on the spot followed various models and were, moreover, executed by artists trained in different schools. Monks, it must be remembered, frequently changed monasteries, and the more gifted ones were either « lent out » or emigrated not to return. Some form of style

3

nevertheless comes to the front in the monasteries famous for their art of illumination which, like every distinctly new manifestation in the history of art, must be due to the personality of some one artist. It is of course impossible in these early times to determine with precision the first manuscript in which the new artistic personality manifested himself, and much less the name of the painter; but we can determine the artist's peculiarities which have been decisive in the style in question. With a uniformity characteristic of the Middle Ages, this style not only extended the strain of its influence to the activity of an entire school, but also to other monastic centers.

We meet occurences of this kind in Reichenau, Fulda, Cologne, Ratisbon, and other places. In the present short survey we shall chiefly follow such stylistic forms, and whenever possible localize them. Considering, however, the present state of research, this will by no means be always possible, and we shall sometimes have to content ourselves with conjectures or a general classification. The growing knowledge of palaeography, which is a constant sister of illumination, will prove particularly helpful.

After the Merovingian initials, composed of fishes, birds, and minor plant formations, had here and there effected their entry upon German soil, a richer decoration with ornamented full pages and figure drawings appears and becomes the fashion under the influence of the Irish and Anglo-Saxon missionary activity. This was subsequently fostered and developed by a further immigration of the so-called Scottish monks, by the introduction of books serving as models, and by the instruction and development of local talent.

In Ireland and England, the existing miniatures were derived from models brought by missionaries from the East and from Italy. This is particularly true on Anglo-Saxon soil where we have to deal with illuminations emanating from the same source as certain continental productions, either because the models had come directly from Syria, Egypt or Byzantium, or because they originated in Lower Italy as a branch of Syro-Egyptian or Byzantine art. But while the models were identical, the manner of imitation adopted in Ireland and England respectively differed from that employed in the so-called Ada

4

group on the Continent. Whereas the Irish illuminators altered their model past all recognition, as for instance in the Syrian type of the draped Christ on the Cross, and simply followed their own bent and inclination for ornamental design, absolutely regardless of any close resemblance to nature, either in the parts or in the whole, the Anglo-Saxons showed a tendency towards more natural representation and kept more closely to their models, although only in a summary manner, for while they reproduced the general appearance, they reduced it to the simplest possible forms. This mode of reproduction was also applied to the chief characteristics of pose and gesture, but failed in carrying out details. As a result of this, the artists had recourse to filling out of the flat parts either by broader and feebler parallel bands following the outline, or by decorative line flourishes. Although here were imitated the same portraits of classical authors seated under arches, which we find reproduced in the miniatures of the Evangelists of the Ada group, there is nevertheless a difference between the two. It lies precisely in the fact that in the former much less attention was paid to details in movement of the outlines and to the differentiation of form design by means of light and shade.

In the beginning the Anglo-Saxon manner was also followed by the German draughtsmen, with the only difference that the latter do not yet show the firmness and uniform skill of their masters. Even more manifest becomes their incapacity when it is a question of mastering pictorial appearances. The artists seem to have grasped to a certain extent the totality of composition and outline, as far as design is concerned, but as soon as it was a question of connecting and constructing the internal parts, of plastic or spatial interpretations, they failed entirely. They simply followed the necessity of filling out spaces, endeavouring to render them vivid and effective by drawing parallel lines or painting coloured bands at different intervals.

It is no mere coincidence that the earliest well-known manuscripts which have come down to us emanate from localities which as early as the time of the Romans had played the most prominent rôle in the West and the East of the German lands, such as Trèves and Salzburg. After the partition of the

Roman Empire, Trèves became one of its capitals and, with Milan, the alternate residence of the Caesars. The wealth, pomp and splendour of the old Imperial city, although it was then only in a state of after-bloom, must have cast their reflection upon the neighbouring abbey of Echternach, founded about 698 by the Anglo-Saxon Willibrord. In the eighth century Echternach had already in its possession a book of the Gospels in the Northumbrian style (Paris, Bibl. Nat. Lat. 9389). The manuscript must either have been brought there or have been locally executed by an Anglo-Saxon (Plate 3) and later on served as a model for the illustrator of another Gospels, now preserved at Trèves (Plate 4), both for the symbols of the Evangelists and the initials. Together with this scribe there worked, however, another draughtsman, of the name of Thomas, who, in his imitation of insular draped figures, reproduced the schematic and summary parallels of the folds in straight and winding lines (Plate 6). On the other hand, the two archangels, holding the frame with the title of the gospel of St. Matthew (Plate 7) point to a Byzantine model and still reflect the naturalistic manner of its drapery motives. And finally, one of the scribes has composed his initials out of fishes and birds, a device hitherto in vogue on the Continent (Plate 8). This manuscript thus gives a clear idea of the collaboration of various draughtsmen and of the variety of models accumulated in such a library. As for the Gospels of the ninth century coming from St. Maria ad Martyres at Trèves (Plates 9 and 10), it exhibits not only a strong Franco-Saxon (Anglo-Frankish) character, particularly in its ornamentation, but also Anglo-Saxon and Byzantine elements.

A Gospels coming from Tegernsee (Munich, Cod. Lat. 19101) betrays in its decorated page, panelled out into four compartments by a cross, a device popular in insular manuscripts (Plate 11). The book, dating from the ninth century, may either have been brought thither from Trèves by the abbot Hartwich, or been imported from Salzburg. Tegernsee, it must be remembered, did not yet exist at that time, whereas at Salzburg the intercourse with the insular style was frequent. Even at this early date Salzburg, the old Juvavum, the foundations of whose ecclesiastical importance were laid by the abbot-bishop Vergilius (743-784), and which became an episcopal see in 798, and extended its sway over the Bavarian bishoprics, had already developed a considerable activity in the execution of artistically decorated manuscripts. It is probably at Salzburg that was executed the Codex Millenarius (Plate 2) now preserved at Kremsmünster, which, in the miniatures of the Evangelists, gives us to some extent an accurate copy of the corresponding figures in the Anglo-Saxon Cutbercht-Gospels (Vienna, Nat. Libr. Cod. 1224) (Plate 1). It was at Salzburg too that the miniature of John Chrysostom (Plate 12) was painted at the beginning of the ninth century under the influence of insular models. In its simplification of a traditional model, this miniature shows in the customary manner the schematic enlivening of the inner parts by means of parallel strokes of the brush. In the same rank may be placed other manuscripts, such as the Vienna Cod. 587 with the miniature of St. Jerome. At the same time, however, we already notice the intrusion of a more pictorial element due to a source more closely approaching the antique, as may be observed in the representations of the months executed at Salzburg, probably in 818 (Plate 13).

In the productions of some monasteries, in particular the Alamannic, such as St. Gall and Reichenau as well as in the Hessian Fulda and at Würzburg, similar insular characteristics at first manifested themselves, soon, however, to make way for direct imitations of Western and Southern models. The latter proceeding may be observed on the two leaves subsequently incorporated in a purple codex written at Augsburg in the ninth century. (Munich, Cim. 2). The illuminations point to productions of the sixth century, but can scarcely themselves date from that time, judging from some peculiarities, particularly of the architecture.

In the subsequent course of the ninth and tenth centuries the influence of the two great early Carolingian schools makes itself felt in the majority of German monasteries. Adopting the classification given by Hubert Janitschek, the two above-mentioned schools are usually designated as the Ada school and the Palace school respectively. The first is clearly so called on account of its stylistic connection with the Ada manuscript preserved at Trèves, while the second, less evidently, derives its name from the Gospels preserved at Vienna together with the imperial insignia and supposed to have come into existence in the neighbourhood of the palace at Aix-la-Chapelle.

It is, however, not yet generally admitted, that the two groups really originated on German soil. This applies both to the group to which belong the Gospels preserved in the Vienna Schatzkammer with its pictorial style approaching the antique, as well as to the Ada manuscript preserved at Trèves, in which a more pronounced oriental style prevails.

The question of the localisation of these schools of illumination is the more important, as they may be said to exhibit most clearly the impress of the opposite poles in the artistic conception of antique forms. The other methods of figure design and drawing of the Carolingian style occupy more or less an intermediate position between the two above mentioned schools. It really seems that both styles had found their starting point in the eastern part of the Frankish Kingdom, on the boundary line separating what subsequently became France, from Germany, and hence extended their activity and influence to the West and the East.

For the pictorial group, and in particular for those manuscripts which most strongly represent its style, tradition points to the Lower Rhine. The Vienna Gospels (Plates 21 and 22) on which the German kings used to take their coronation oath is supposed to have been discovered by Otto III on the knees of Charlemagne when the former had the Emperor's sepulchre opened. A second Gospel manuscript is an old possession of the treasury-chamber of the cathedral at Aix-la-Chapelle (Plate 23), a third, preserved in the library at Brussels (no. 18723), comes from Xanten, while a fourth, reproducing the Vienna miniatures of the Evangelists and preserved at Berlin (Cod. theol. lat. fol. 260), comes from Clèves (Plate 24). The subsequent influence of this style is furthermore particularly noticeable in the Franco-Belgian district and in the scriptoria of Cologne in the tenth and eleventh centuries, so that we can scarcely avoid the conjecture that these miniatures are the work of an illuminator who had his atelier in the centre of these parts, namely in Charlemagne's court at Aix-la-Chapelle. Reims has been claimed as the place of origin of these illustrations, because the manuscripts executed under archbishop Ebo of Reims exhibit a similar artistic style of illumination. It must, however, be borne in mind that it was precisely this prelate who is said to have been for some time the director of the Imperial Library at Aix-la-Chapelle. We may therefore quite well imagine that it was the archbishop Ebo who transplanted both the method and its supporters to Reims where it was continued in the Gospels executed by himself (now preserved at Epernay), in the Utrecht-Psalter and other works.

But, however that may be, the pictorial style of painting, most strongly represented by the above mentioned manuscripts, constitutes at all events one of the foundations upon which subsequent German decoration of books was based. In the first place we have manuscripts of a secular character, dealing with astronomy, natural science and medicine, where the illuminations are derived from the same style and by their contents also point to a classical source. It is possible that we also have to reckon with the Greek Renaissance movement after the iconoclastic storm, and it is quite conceivable that the models of the Gospels at Vienna and Aix-la-Chapelle originated in that milieu the style of which, approaching the antique, had reappeared in all probability as soon as towards the end of the eighth century, if indeed it had not survived from the Early Christian period, as appears probable from indications in Santa Maria Antiqua in Rome. Lower Italy too deserves special consideration, for there the influence of the Eastern Roman Empire was particularly strong. There we constantly meet the Greek language and Greek styles in contact with the Mediterranean coasts. Was it not precisely from Lower Italy that the missionaries brought Greek models to the British Islands where they were made the basis for Irish and Anglo-Saxon book decoration, just as soon afterwards they were used in France?

As evidence not only of Greek models but as a positive proof of a Greek artist, it has been pointed out that the name of « Demetrius Presbyter », unusual in the Occident, is inscribed in contemporary chrysography on the border of the first page of St. Luke in the Vienna Gospels. There is, however, no indication that the name refers to either the scribe or the illustrator.

The absence of the apocalyptic symbols in the representation of the Evangelists agrees with the Byzantine custom. Generally speaking, we can observe a scarcity of ornament in this group of manuscripts, while, on the contrary, decoration occupies a particularly large space in the other scriptoria of the time. This absence of ornaments, like the plastically conceived framework surrounding the miniatures, echoes the antique spirit, whereas the books replete with ornamentation differ widely in figure design from the pictorial character of the antique style.

Opposed to the School of the Palace entirely pictorial in its origin and supposed to have made its first appearance at Aix-la-Chapelle, is another style which, after all, in its first point of departure, may perhaps be traced to similar Greek sources, but had already undergone a transformation within the confines of the Roman Empire, namely in Syria, and then, either directly or after a transplantation to Lower Italy, penetrated first into England and under Charlemagne into the Frankish Kingdom. We are referring to the group of miniatures which, deriving their name from one of its principal representatives, the Ada manuscript of Trèves, are called the Ada group. This group is all the more important as it offered the best opportunities for a development in the purely mediaeval artistic conception and is consequently, as far as filiation is concerned, of even greater importance than the more retrospective pictorial school.

To the Ada group belongs a whole series of magnificent manuscripts very closely connected with Charlemagne and the Imperial family, so that they must have been executed in a place which was in close connection with the court. This group includes the Evangelistary written for Charlemagne by Godescalc in the years 781-783 (Paris, lat. 1203) (Plates 25-28), the Psalter written by Dagulf before 795 as a gift of Charlemagne to Pope Hadrian (Vienna, Cod. 1861), the Ada Gospels of Trèves (Plate 29), a present of

Ada who was supposed to have been a sister of Charlemagne and who gave her name to the style of the entire group. To the Ada group further belong a Gospel manuscript at Abbeville coming from the monastery of St. Riquier, where it was preserved and said to have been sent by Charlemagne to his relative Abbot Angilbert (790-814) (Plates 42-44), and lastly, a manuscript coming from St. Médard at Soissons (Paris, lat. 8850) (Plates 31-34). It is traditionally alleged that the last named manuscript is the « artistic » Gospels which King Louis the Débonnaire gave as a present to the Church of St. Médard at Easter, together with other ecclesiastical utensils. As the latter bore the monogram of Charlemagne, it may rightly be assumed that the man-uscript had also come from the legacy of that Emperor. To the above series, for which external evidence points to Charlemagne, may be added on pure-ly artistic grounds many other manuscripts. Such are the Gospels in Lon-don (Harley 2788) (Plates 35-37), the Gospels from Lorsch, half of which is preserved in the Vatican (Pal. 50) and half at Karlsburg in Roumania (Plates 38-41), the Gospels at Munich, Gotha (Plates 46-48), Manchester, Paris (Cod. Lat. 8849) (Plate 45), etc.

The figures of the Ada group are mostly limited to the portraits of the Evangelists, grandiosely enthroned on chairs, the seats and backs of which are covered with cushions and draperies. With their Gospels in their hands or placed in front of them on the desk, they are busy writing or sharpening their pens, examining or dipping them into the inkhorn. With these vari-ations their pose is either full face or in profile, and their gaze is correspond-ingly turned either to the observer, concentrated upon their occupation, or raised to their respective symbols whence they draw inspiration. The latter fill the entire tympanum, the upper part of the pillared arch which, richly orna-mented with curtains or architectural designs, frames the enthroned author. Here and there we also find a few other full page illuminations, such as the enthroned Christ of the youthful beardless type, the Fountain of Life, or the Apocalyptical vision of the lamb and the twenty-four Elders, as well as rich canon-tables and initials.

Evidently the style of the figure painting must have been derived from a prototype itself already derived from still earlier models, for it consists of two quite divergent elements. On the one hand, we have a coloured modelling style which is particularly noticeable in the flesh parts, while on the other, there is a firm outlining of the forms, not only exhibited in the cast of the drapery and in its fidgetted edges, but also surrounding the face, hands and feet, and even definitely fixing the details of the face. It is a style derived from the antique illusionistic technique, and which in its search for an established pattern, finds it chiefly in the firm demarcation of the objective and in a colour canon. The latter may particularly be observed in the fixed formula according to which the heads are drawn. Dark brown and black are used for the lines of the eyebrows and of the upper eyelids, the iris, the nostrils and the corners of the mouth; red for the line between eyebrow and eyelid, the lower parts of the nose, the oral fissure and one side line of the bridge of the nose, while the other side of the nose and the lower eyelids are coloured in a green or greyish green tint, which sometimes even verges into a bluish green. This canon has become an established rule and indicates the close connection between different members of the group of manuscripts in question.

If we now enquire after the source of such a pattern, we find it in the Eastern Roman Empire. The heads on the mosaics of Kahr-Hiram near Tyre, dating from the sixth century and preserved in the Louvre, exhibit an identical pattern which still survives in Byzantine mosaics of the twelfth century. Janitschek has already called attention to the relations existing between the small figure scenes in the Soissons Gospels and those of the Syrian Rabula Gospels of the sixth century. It is also an early Syrian manuscript, the Gospels of Etsch-miadzin, which precisely shows the not yet otherwise existing series of miniatures with the Fountain of Life, such as we meet in the Godescalc Evangelistary and in the Gospels of Soissons belonging to the Ada group. The peculiar projecting and retreating architectural backgrounds of the Soissons Gospels with the numerous windowed stories also appear, in a feebler ren-

12

dering, in the miniatures of the Evangelists found in the Armenian manuscript of Queen Mlke, dating from 900 and preserved in San Lazzaro near Venice. The Syrian source of the Ada group is thus almost certain. The objection that no corresponding model has been preserved and, in particular, no analogous accentuation of the symbols of the Evangelists, is no counter-evidence, if we remember how few are the early Syrian manuscripts which have come down to us. The introduction of the symbols might belong to a South Italian transformation. A reflection of such decorated pages is found in the miniature of the enthroned Luke with the great symbol in the lunette of the so-called Augustine manuscript at Cambridge (Corpus Christi College, Cod. 286). The latter, which probably was illuminated in Lower Italy at the beginning of the seventh century, is treated in a purely linear manner. The productions, however, of the Ada group are not the result of a more plastic and colour-modelled copy of such an original, but must be traced to an earlier prototype. The proof is to be found in the above mentioned colour system, which is precisely one of the results of the later antique East Roman transformation. It also lies in the fact that precisely the coloured modelling surpassing that of the Augustine manuscript just referred to, is something very alien to and mostly not understood by mediaeval occidental artists. It can therefore only be considered as an inheritance.

From historical sources we know that within the confines of the Carolingian Empire numerous Syrians were found and that they played a considerable rôle, particularly as far as commercial relations were concerned.

With regard to ornamentation, other sources also claim attention. Rich and complicated plaitwork, out of which the initials are composed, was developed on Irish and Anglo-Saxon soil and transplanted to the Continent, where the leafwork, inherited from classical times, was added. And here one can rightly speak of a style peculiar to the Ada group. Probably on account of the drawing pen, it abounds in cellular partitions and rake or comblike designs of leaves, particularly in the capitals approaching the Corinthian order, which harmonize so well with the plaitwork. In accordance with the oriental character, the tints are variegated and heavy, while the lights, in accordance with the covering character of the technique, are heightened and brightened with a wash of white pigment. Gold is also lavishly used, especially in the ornamentation, here and there also in the drapery, but never as a background. This constitutes a significant contrast with the manuscripts of the tenth century.

In addition to these devices, antique gems are imitated by white figures on a small scale, and twisted pillars ornamented with similar small human figures. In the spandrels or on the canon-tables appear birds and trees naturalistically rendered.

A number of circumstances make it probable that this school of painting had originated on German soil. The particular saints mentioned in the pericopes of the earliest manuscript, the Godescalc Evangeliary, are Maximinus, Bonifacius, and Nazarius, a circumstance which points to Trèves, Fulda and Lorsch. Ada, surnamed « ancilla dei », a supposed sister of Charlemagne, who was the originator of the Ada manuscript, was buried in St. Maximinus at Trèves. She had made gifts both to Fulda and Lorsch. At all events, we are moving in this East Frankish circle in which Trèves, as an important centre, occupies a particularly predominant position. As for the neighbouring monastery of Echternach, it played an important rôle as early as in the eighth century. The peculiar decorative motives of the Gospels executed there, (treasury of the cathedral at Trèves, Cod. 61 [134]) such as the small coloured rosettes, are repeated in the Gospels of St. Maria ad Martyres at Trèves, dating from the ninth century (Municipal Library Cod. 23), which in the drawing and design of the heads exhibits the colour system of the Ada school (Plate 9), and also in its Comes it agrees with that of the Ada manuscript itself, just as does the Lectionary of the neighbouring monastery of Prüm, written in the eleventh century (Manchester, Rylands Lib. No. 7).

The reputation of Trèves, the former capital of the western half of the Empire, had somewhat declined, but under Charlemagne, who had raised it to an archbishopric, the city once more regained its former importance. It is therefore highly probable that it was at Trèves that the Ada manuscript was

14

executed, although there is no sure proof for such an assertion. At all events as everything points to the present-day German portion of the Frankish Empire, the description of this group deserves a special place in a history of German painting.

Nor were the centres situated on French soil, where the art of manuscript illumination was practised, without importance for Germany. As such, one may mention the scriptorium of Tours which owed its influence to the activity of the great teacher Alcuin, although he probably concentrated his attention upon the correctness of the text and the scientific contents of the books rather than upon their ornamentation. Nevertheless, during the following decades the criticism of the text was succeeded by attention especially paid to the decoration of magnificent manuscripts. It is also quite certain that the numerous disciples of the great Anglo-Saxon scholar, who occupied the posts of abbots in many German monasteries, frequently fetched their texts and illustrations from the mother-monastery. The influence makes itself thus felt at Fulda, St. Gall and Trèves. The style of figure drawing prevalent at Tours does not occupy such an important position as that of either the Ada group or the Gospels in the Vienna Schatzkammer. Its place is rather intermediary between the two, and as regards technical execution, the love of drawing transforms the pictorial style without dissolving it entirely.

While in the case of the introduction of the style from Tours, we have to do with an occasional importation from the centre of France, the activity of another school in neighbouring districts made itself steadily felt. It penetrated in particular into the regions of the Lower Rhine and hence farther into Germany. It is the so-called Franco-Saxon style, at home in the North-East of France and in Belgium. It principally consisted of a fusion of the Anglo-Saxon and Continental elements, the insular factors predominating in ornament and the continental pictorial characteristics in the figure drawing. As an indication of Anglo-Saxon influence may also be considered the symbols of the Evangelists framed in circles (Plate 49), in particular when, like other circular miniatures (Plate 5), they cut the arch.

Finally, according to the latest research of A. M. Friend, the products of all the schools seem to have met in the scriptorium of Charles the Bald at St. Denis and to have given rise to a particularly rich style which has hitherto been wrongly attributed to the monastery of Corbie. It may of course be assumed that when works executed in this style penetrated into Germany they did not fail to exercise an influence, as examples in Ratisbon and in St. Gall will show us, but one cannot speak in this case of any steady introduction of a school.

If we consider the sudden appearance of the different styles, especially the Ada group and the Palace school, and observe the later decline in quality, we might conclude from this fact that under the rule of Charlemagne not only men of science, but also artists were invited from abroad. The latter were probably chiefly Italians by whom were developed the indigenous talents who subsequently continued the traditions on their own account.

At the same time an effort is frequently made to produce with pen and ink alone the same effects as with brush and colour. This was the natural result of the fact that the art of illumination had now fallen almost entirely into the hands of scribes, whereas at first for more important works special painters were most likely employed. The latter, considering illuminating art, and perhaps also monumental painting, as their particular profession, may possibly also have executed the mural paintings in the edifices of Charlemagne and of Louis le Débonnaire. It is doubtful whether in every case the illuminators were monks. On the contrary, certain texts and representations of artists point to the fact that even secular painters sometimes executed illuminations.

The change of the coloured models, painted with a covering technique, into drawings executed with the pen or even a fine brush, was effected with two purposes in view. What the artist mostly aimed at in the beginning, was to produce the coloured character as far as possible by means of thick strokes often intertwisting and running into each other, and by a quick movement of the hand running backwards and forwards, as is the case in France, especially in the school of Reims. As for Germany, we have examples of this method in the Freising Gospels coming from Schäftlarn (Plate 50) and in the Weltenburg Gospels (Plate 51).

Another manner did not renounce the variety of colours and developed a coloured drawing. That is to say, it adopted a technical treatment which consisted in the following execution: instead of continuously laying on the colour on the surface and then proceeding with the modelling, the illuminator drew with a thick or fine brush coloured outlines, filling them in by means of multiplied parallel strokes, which by the difference of colours, alternating repeatedly their tints, gave a more variegated effect, without, however, producing actual modelling. As examples of this style may be mentioned the Gospel manuscript from Innichen in the Tyrol (Plate 52) or St. Paul's Epistles at Munich (Plate 53). In other respects, the characteristics of the latter manuscript point mostly to the Ada group.

Gradually, however, the illuminators freed themselves from this enforced imitation and attain a pure and firm style in linear drawing. They try to produce their effect by gracefully curved lines, a wealth of distinctly expressed motives and a premeditated alternation of broad and narrow bands, and thus attain to create something new, independently of the models. This faculty increases, especially during the latter half of the ninth century, all through the tenth century and down to the eleventh. It seems to have flourished above all in the Swiss monasteries, in Fulda and in central Germany whence it penetrated into northern Germany. The specimens reproduced on Plates 81-87 afford a clear idea of this manner.

A further change from the enforced imitation of traditional models, as may be noticed in the miniatures of the Evangelists in the Ada group, was effected in the sphere of composition. The position and cast of drapery of the enthroned figures are either varied or combined, but this process, which at first takes place within the limits of the traditional models, gradually becomes independent in its arrangements. The symbols are placed in new positions, by the side or above the Evangelists, new desks are invented, architectural designs are added, and the filling-in of the flat surface shows an independent disposition. A

17

particularly striking example of this manner is afforded by the Gospels coming from Innichen and preserved at Innsbruck (Plate 52).

The drapery motives, transmitted in the early models as inventions of the classical past, become established rules which are being constantly repeated and combined in various ways by the mediaeval illuminator. While, however, the artist familiarises himself with the patterns to such an extent that he is able to reproduce them in an analogous but independent manner, he generally fails to find a new interpretation where nature is concerned. Nor do the illuminators in Germany during the early Carolingian period show such an independence in stylising human figures as do for instance the Irish scribes. They succeed, however, in pure ornamentation, as the more decorative sphere does not check the flight of their imagination as much as the human figure. It is only in secondary details and accessories of the folds of the drapery that this decorative impulse prevails and busies itself in the reproduction of fluttering ends, moving edges and symmetrical folds. Thus the cast of drapery of the figures in the Apolcalypse of Trèves (Plate 54) differs in no way from the motives of classical drapery, and only in the ends of the cloth fluttering down from the book of the angel has the draughtsman added something of his own. But even here he has taken for his basis a classical formula. In the drapery of the Evangelists in a Paris Manuscript (Plate 45), the folds positively seem to be entangled.

On the other hand, in the sphere of pure ornamentation, in the decorated pages, in initials and in the frames of the miniatures, the illuminators manifest a greater freedom. It cannot be said that they are great innovators, but they prove at all events to be clever manipulators of the traditional elements of plaitwork, of fantastic animals and of classical leaf-work and foliage. Those they utilize in rich variations and with a wonderfully fine dynamic sense. It is especially in the conception of depth of space that the illuminator seemed to lack sensitiveness and imagination, and whenever perspective exists in the models, we find a constant deviation. We have only to compare the illuminations accompanying the handing over by the scribe of the work of Hrabanus

Maurus (Plate 55). In the Vienna copy of the original, which had evidently been provided with illustrations in the time of the author, as they were indispensable for the text, the different spacial positions occupied by the participants are observed more faithfully than in the Vatican copy. Whereas in the former manuscript the monks present are placed on both sides behind the abbot's chair, in the latter copy we see them in a row by the side of the chair. At the same time the graphic element in the Vatican manuscript predominates over the pictorial. Among the miniatures of this manuscript we also find the portrait of Louis le Débonnaire in the equipment of a Christian warrior, an illumination which, like other figure reproductions in this work, is covered with a number of complicated inscriptions. (Plate 56).

The activity at Fulda seems to have been particularly prolific. The abbot Hrabanus Maurus, called «praeceptor Germaniae», was a disciple of Alcuin, and evidently introduced customs from Tours into his monastery. In addition models of all sorts accumulated in the library, and later Roman inventions, partly through England, partly from the centre of the Ada group, exercised their influence. Fulda, it must be remembered, was founded by the Anglo-Saxon Boniface, and as the Anglo-Saxon writing was at home there for a long time, many specimens of insular illumination may either have been executed or preserved in the scriptorium. As a result, the productions of the local artists vary considerably. Among the illuminators at Fulda who were active during the first half of the ninth century are mentioned Bruun, Rodulph and Modestus, the first of whom seems to have practised monumental as well as miniature painting. To classical models the illustrations of the Agrimensores, a collection of treatises dealing with land surveying, seem to point most directly. The meeting of the nine scholars (Plate 16A) is, of course, rather clumsily represented, but it is evident that it is based upon the illusionistic pictorial style, which is expressed more purely in the half-length portrait, that, according to a late note, is supposed to represent the Emperor as protector (Plate 16B). A closer imitation of the model is even more evident in the miniature of Terence (Plate 17) which precedes a manuscript of his comedies. The copy was preserved at

19

the beginning of the ninth century in the monastery of Corvey and was either executed on the spot by a monk named Aldricus or brought by him from the French mother cloister of Corbie, when Corvey was founded. How differently the models, probably belonging to the fifth and sixth centuries, could be reproduced will become clear from a comparison of the different scenes pictured in this manuscript with those found in one coming from St. Denis (Plate 18). The illuminator of the latter manuscript had copied the same model but altered the coloured miniatures into linear drawings.

It is significant that the manuscripts of a secular nature showed the strongest tendency to retain the pictorial style of their prototypes. Here one strove to acquire foreign wisdom as accurately as possible, whereas religious conceptions belonged more strongly to the events of everyday life. To an astronomical encyclopedia belongs the celestial chart (Plate 14) found in a manuscript executed at Salzburg, probably written in 818 and preserved as early as the tenth century in St. Emmeram at Ratisbon. In addition to the separate constellations (Plate 15), it contains a representation of the twelve months. The illuminations are better executed in another manuscript coming from Salzburg, produced between 809 and 821 (Plate 13). To judge from certain indications, the model must have come from the north of France, and one may surely conclude that its execution was in the pictorial style. In general, there is more than one copy extant of most of these works, frequently a whole series. The copies may be said to bear to one another the relation of a family with many branches, whose genealogical tree scholars are endeavouring to establish and whose ancestor was frequently the only immigrant from the South to the North. One may conclude from this how many works never made the journey across the Alps or the sea and disappeared entirely, without leaving any offspring.

An important rôle was also played by medical works, either of an anatomical or pharmaceutical character. In the rank of the last named belong the books dealing with plants and their sanative virtues, such as the Dioscorides and the Apuleius. Among the works known under this name and that of

Musa, a physician of Augustus, may be counted a manuscript of the tenth century, now at Cassel, which was possibly executed at Fulda and which in its miniatures still exhibits all the characteristics of its southern Italian proto-type (Plates 19 and 20).

The illuminations of the liturgical manuscripts of Fulda are, on the other hand, executed in a more precise decorative style, particularly the title pages of the Gospels. Like those of Würzburg (Plate 57) and Erlangen (Plate 58), they betray a complete dependence upon the Ada group, showing most strongly a severe training derived from its starting point. The same fundamental elements reappear in the pose of the Evangelists, in the drapery of the throne, in the ar-chitectural framing and in the detailed representation of the symbolical animals in an easily alternating decorative connection. The great mantle motive of the St. Luke in Würzburg (Plate 57) which is also derived from the classical style is changed here into an ornamental curve. The endeavour to produce strong characteristic heads and precise modelling, in spite of the firmness of the out-lines, points to a rather close vicinity to the old models. Much feebler appear the later derivations of the tenth century, particularly noticeable in the Codex Wittechindeus at Berlin which also originated at Fulda (Plate 60). In this manuscript the forms, irregular and petty, aim more strongly at that linear play which develops a purer style in other works of the same period.

In the ornamentation of the initials, these Fulda manuscripts, in which green, blue, and violet tints predominate, show delicate natural plant forma-tions and tendrils with coloured lights on a darker ground, unusual in Caro-lingian ornamental motives. The Evangelistary of the Munich University Li-brary, evidently written at Fulda (Plate 59), is an example of this style.

Hrabanus Maurus, who had spread Carolingian culture over vast German areas, considered the study of pagan authors as indispensable, and laid par-ticular stress upon the value of artistic works. It may therefore be assumed that the influence of Fulda was strong in miniature painting, especially as its monks frequently attained the dignity of abbot in other German monasteries.

As for the artistic activity of Mainz, Lorsch and Würzburg, which presumably were related to Fulda, our information is still too scant to warrant any safe assertions. Nevertheless, it is from Lorsch, where it was probably executed, that a miscellaneous Codex in the Vatican comes. This manuscript contains a peculiar pen drawing of the Trinity (Plate 61) which, in its drapery, still exhibits an alliance with the Ada group. Another page in this manuscript representing the Crucifixion, seems to be closely allied to a similar miniature in the Concordance of the Gospels Otfried of Weissenburg (Plate 62). The latter manuscript must probably have been executed in the latter half of the ninth century, in the not far distant Benedictine monastery on the boundary of the Palatinate. Closely allied to this manuscript is also a Crucifixion, subsequently incorporated in a Psalter of northern French origin in Berlin which is dedicated to a certain Ludovicus Rex (Plate 63).

Whether the « Presbyter Samuhel », to whom we owe several illuminated manuscripts (Plates 65 and 66), is identical with the friend and disciple of Hrabanus, who was for a short time abbot of Lorsch, is doubtful. But at any rate, initials and miniatures of the Evangelists are allied to French works, and many details, such as the small soaring symbols in the Maihingen manuscript, lead us to assume intercourse with Tours.

Besides Fulda, the « Alamannic » monasteries exercised the strongest influence in fostering literary and artistic interests, and in the first rank are to be counted St. Gall and Reichenau. Whereas the school of Reichenau seems to have reached a flourishing state only under the Saxon Emperors, important productions of the artistic activity of St. Gall, in particular during the ninth century, have come down to us.

Richly illuminated Irish manuscripts are still preserved in the monastery founded by St. Gall, who accompanied the Irish missionary Columbanus in the seventh century. A pronounced artistic skill seems, however, only to have flourished under the influence of French monastic schools, when Abbot Gozbert (816-837), paid particular attention to the library. Although in his time the decoration of manuscripts was still restrained and in the old-fashioned Merovingian manner, we meet an exceedingly rich ornamentation in the Psalter executed by the monk Folchard, who flourished under abbot Grimvald (841-872), a disciple of Alcuin. Here Carolingian and transmitted Irish elements intermingle, and the classical acanthus leafwork and foliage and Corinthian-ized capitals appear side by side with Irish spirals and convolutions and Ca-rolingian plaitwork (Plate 71). Although one still notices a borrowing from the various Carolingian scriptoria, the ornamentation of the initials made an independent step forward and proved of considerable importance both for its development during the tenth century and its influence on wide areas of book decoration. Floral tendril work is allied to abstract band plaiting, and the small buds or branches, and occasionally half palmettes, issuing from the loosening band, tend to give the formal knots something of the character of plants (Plate 70A). The patterns have a more robust appearance than the work of the French schools. A vigorous colour scheme of vermilion, green and blue is contrasted with gold and silver on purple grounds. In the Golden Psalter executed about a decade later this variegation is still increased, and in the equestrian groups (Plate 69) red, green and violet horses stand side by side. Cheek by jowl with miniatures such as those of the Psalmist David with his musicians and dancers (Plate 68A), borrowed from the Psalter of Charles the Bald (Plate 68B) and symmetrically doubled, there appear others, illus-trating the life of David, evidently due to free invention. It is in particular such lively scenes of warlike activity which seem to have been the joy of the illuminators of St. Gall, for it was in the same circle that were executed the numerous battles of the Maccabeans which fill a manuscript preserved at Ley-den (Plates 72 and 73). Such are also the allegorical battles in the Psychoma-chia of Prudentius, among whose numerous replicas the most lively, the Bern manuscript, was probably executed at St. Gall a generation later (Plates 74 and 75).

One notices that the illuminator was anxious to make his figures appear life-like and vigorous. The movements are clearly set off, and stress is laid upon the muscles; the hips, chest and body are drawn with exaggerated roundness, while the heads have an energetic appearance. In like manner, too, the miniatures representing the Months in the Wandalbert Martyrology at Rome (Plate 76), which were surely borrowed from a later classical prototype, receive their particular stamp adapted to the taste of the time. In all these miniatures which we examined the covering colouring is neglected, stress being laid upon the drawing which is only more or less lightly covered with patches of colour. The parchment thus frequently remains bare, and the colour becomes evident only in the shaded parts which, as in the Golden Psalter, are added in brush strokes. The miniature of the penitent David, belonging to the ninth century, which was probably also executed at St. Gall (Plate 77) forms an exception to this rule. Here the worshipping King reminds us of the corresponding figure in the Paris Psalter Grec. 139 with its classical Byzantine illuminations. In contrast, however, to this miniature, the colour is frequently entirely abandoned and the drawing becomes the more expressive. The St. Gall Derision of St. Paul (Plate 78), which was possibly executed by the same draughtsman as the Prudentius, represents the mocking of the Apostle who is standing in a statue-like attitude, upon a pedestal. In power of expression it leaves nothing to be desired. In the vigorous, although somewhat roughly drawn St. Paul writing (Plate 79) we get a glimpse of a model of the Ada group, but the colouring, with the exception of a few insignificant touches with the brush, is abandoned. Coloured illustrations of scientific works, such as the constellations and celestial charts, are now also transcribed in mere outline-drawings (Plate 80).

Thus the attraction of a large group of illuminations from the ninth to the eleventh centuries lies in the manner in which the pen drawing tries to make use of its own means of activity. Plates 81 to 87 reproduce miniatures of this uniform style, although it cannot be safely asserted that all the examples were executed in the same scriptorium. It is even impossible to say with any degree of certainty which localities had a share in the execution of these illuminations. Fulda and the Alamannic monasteries, however, once more appear in the foreground of probability.

The Feast of Pentecost, one of the representations contained in the Evangelistary at Cassel coming from the monastery of Abdinghof near Paderborn (Plate 82), has served as a model for the pen drawing (Plate 83B) in a sacramentary manuscript produced for the monastery of Corvey and executed either on the spot or at Fulda. The drawing, however, only reproduces the upper part of the model, namely the dove of the Holy Ghost between the two angels. On the other hand, we find that a similarity in the treatment of the forms evidently exists between the Majestas Domini from Abdinghof (Plate 81) and the Aesculapius miniature of the Herbarium (Plate 19A) which may possibly have been made at Fulda, though it is executed in colours. The style of the miniatures of the Evangelists (Plate 83A) in an Evangelistary coming from Magdeburg also agrees with the Fulda-Corvey drawing, as does also a manuscript of the Gospels preserved in the library of Wolfenbüttel (Plates 85 and 86). And finally, the Bremen Evangelistary at Munich (Vol. II, Plate 89) exhibits a similar, although coloured style of execution. The latter, as also the crucifix of the Corvey manuscript just mentioned (Vol. II, Plate 111) shows the more pictorial parallels of such pen drawings.

Whether the pen drawings in a manuscript preserved at Leipzig (Plate 84), in view of the fact that it is bound together with a fragment whose ornamented initials surely point to Reichenau, were also executed at Reichenau, is doubtful. But manuscripts of Einsiedeln and the Christ enthroned in Majesty found in a manuscript at Zürich (Plate 87), as well as the Ruodprecht group of Reichenau (cf. Vol. II) represent the style in the Swiss monasteries. Judging from provenance and place of preservation, it would seem that outside of South Germany this style was especially at home in the districts of the Weser, from Fulda to Corvey and Westphalia as far as Bremen and is also reflected in some of the Saxon works.

In any case, the style must be considered as the result of an independent elaboration of old traditional motives. It displays firmness and precision in the line-strokes, effects of shading by means of curving lines broadened into stripes, or by a fusion of thickly laid on ink shadowings. We further notice agitated ruffled edges, fluttering ends, folds floating in parallel curves and,

25

what is most striking, parts of the body which are plastically prominent, such as the muscles of arms and limbs, the stomach and the knees strongly accentuated, sharply set off and encircled by folds. Although the figures need not necessarily have been copied exactly from antique models, the motives of the single parts are all of classical origin, of the same kind as those which served as prototypes for the Ada group and other Carolingian schools. This method, which secures in a certain way an impression of the body, and leaves free play to the garment, may also be noticed in the Winchester manuscripts which were equally derived from Carolingian painting. The style continues on German soil as late as the eleventh century. It is also reflected in sculpture which borrowed its designs and patterns from painting. The fact that the Byzantine illuminators had arrived at like results deserves particular notice, and the similar tracing of the smooth protruding parts of the body in Venetian and Sicilian mosaics is very striking. The style seems therefore to be the natural result of the schematizing of antique draped figures, which in the hands of German draughtsmen assumes a particularly pronounced ornamental character and is consciously utilized for this purpose.

From all that has been said above, the following conclusions may be drawn: Carolingian illumination is not to be considered as a new art which had grown up on the native soil of the Frankish Empire. It was not the result of a slow preparation and gradually increasing skill, but was an art consciously imported, imitating foreign models, and endeavouring to learn something which it had hitherto ignored. In his new residence at Aix-la-Chapelle, Charlemagne, feeling himself to be the successor of the great Germanic ruler Theodoric in Italy, evoked the memory of the edifices erected by that prince. He had his palace-chapel built after the style of San Vitale in Ravenna, and in front of his residence he erected the equestrian statue supposed to be that of the King of the Ostrogoths. In like manner he had decided that the art of painting should flourish in his lands as it had in Italy.

In contrast to the productions of the Merovingian age, most clumsy in their technical execution, Carolingian book-decoration, of which we possess sufficient examples, strives to follow very closely the style and technique of classical models and prototypes. This statement may equally be applied to monumental painting, although the scarcity of extant monuments does not permit any sure judgment.

But in this imitation of antique models, particularly in the ornamental decoration, individual ability and skill make themselves felt. They are of an abstracting nature and either entirely overlook the figure design and natural likeness, or transform them in the sense of pure line or colour dynamics. Although the greatest share in the transformation must be attributed to Irish and Anglo-Saxon art, the draughtsmen in the Frankish Kingdom, adopting this, developed it in their own manner, their gaze, however, being in a higher degree directed upon classical art and its realistic elements of ornament. It is in the north that the initial was above all independently developed, for it was unknown to the antique book as a motive of sumptuous decoration. It developed until its ornamentations filled entire pages, adapting even representations of the human figure to its linear designs and fillings. For many centuries one may still observe the difference from Oriental and Byzantine manuscripts into which the ornamental initial had likewise been introduced. Whereas in the latter in accordance with the Greek spirit, the figure-design always constitutes a naturally formed addition to the letter, important as regards contents, in the West it mostly is quite swallowed up by the ornamental pattern and often becomes a mere play of the imagination without any value for the illustration of the text.

In the Carolingian period the figure scene as taken from the model still remained comparatively intact, but already there are indications of circumstances foreshadowing a new development. In the first place, there are the technical peculiarities which belong to book-decoration in particular and are connected with pen drawing and colouring. To these we must add the desire of the followers of the new culture to accentuate in their expressions the clearness of the narrative in contradistinction to optical veracity. The symbols of this new expression are clearly developed only in the Ottonian period where also the line-

27

ar drawing attains its established form for the first time. The latter, however, may be considered both as a distinct result of the attempts made in the Carolingian age and as a goal at first not yet clearly perceived, but towards which the instinct of natural independence had been steering from the start. Therefore, these later forms were allowed to be described in connection with their most important starting point, Carolingian painting.

INDEX

PLATES 1-88

I

VIENNA, NATIONALBIBLIOTHEK. Cod. 1224 (23,8 x 31 cm)

CUTBERCHT GOSPELS

Eighth century (about 770) written by a South-English scribe Cutbercht, perhaps in Salzburg (?). The MS. was already at Salzburg in the first half of the ninth century.

FOL. 17ᵛ: THE EVANGELIST MATTHEW

Vellum ground. Light colours thinly laid on: blue and lilac with lines in minium (under-garment and top of desk), brownish lilac with brown interior lines (cloak, hair and beard), light ochre with minium (skin over the chair), minium (foot of chair and lamp). The same tints with the addition of pale green in the frame. The flesh tints are pink brown with more vigorously red lips, spots on the cheeks and shades. The space for lights uncoloured.

BIBLIOGRAPHY

HERMANN, I, p. 50 ff. Plates XI-XX, coloured plate.
SWARZENSKI, II, p. 1 ff.
ZIMMERMANN, *Vorkarol. Min.*, p. 30, 128, 137 ff. 297 ff., Plates 297-312.

2

KREMSMÜNSTER, STIFTSBIBLIOTHEK
CIM. I. COD. MILLENARIUS (20 x 30,2 cm)
GOSPELS

Probably from Salzburg; about 860; was at Kremsmünster as early as the eleventh century, according to an indication in the inventory.

A. FOL. 17ᵛ: THE EVANGELIST MATTHEW

Undergarment blue with yellow borders. Upper garment violet. Hair bluish grey. Flesh-tints pink with dark red shades and brown drawing.

B. FOL. 18: SYMBOL OF ST. MATTHEW

The cloak is white, undergarment violet and red. Tints of the flesh as in A. (cf. Janitschek).

BIBLIOGRAPHY

ADA-HS. p. 103 ff., Plates 37-38.
ARNETH, p. 23 ff.
HERMANN, I, p. 50 f.
SWARZENSKI, II. p. 4 ff. There will also be found a detailed description, numerous bibliography and small reproductions not given by Janitschek in the Ada-Hs.
ZIMMERMANN, *Vorkarol. Min.,* p. 137 f.

from Ada-Hs., plate 37 and 38

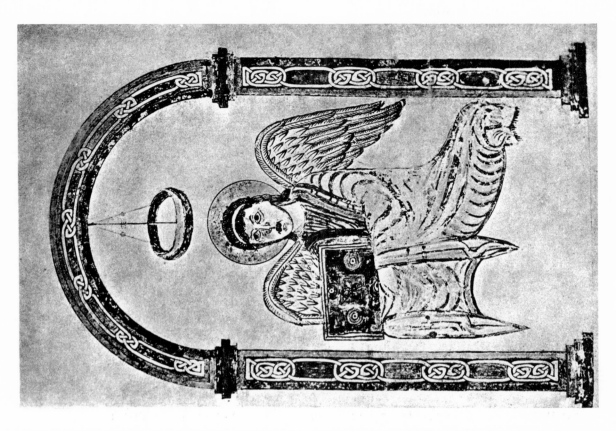
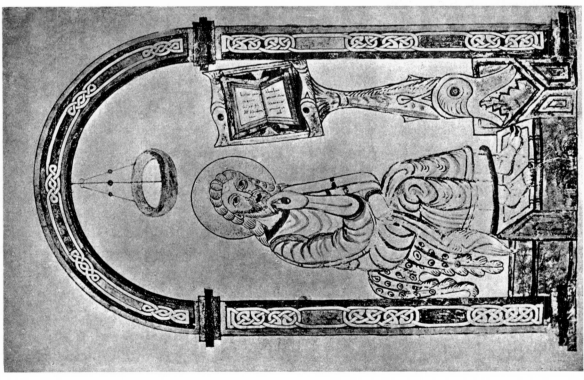

3

PARIS, BIBLIOTHÈQUE NATIONALE. Cod. lat. 9389
(25 x 33,7 cm)
GOSPELS FROM ECHTERNACH

By a North English painter (either executed in or imported to Echter-nach) by the middle of eighth century.

A. FOL. 115ᵛ: SYMBOL OF ST. LUKE

The bull is yellow and pink with black outline and dots, the frame is light vermilion.

B. FOL. 176ᵛ: SYMBOL OF ST. JOHN

Colours as in A. The feathers are light brown touched with scarlet-vermilion (cf. ZIMMERMANN).

BIBLIOGRAPHY

ZIMMERMANN, *Vorkarol. Min.*, p. 122 ff., 276 f., Plates 255-58. Ibid. further bibliographical references.

from Zimmermann, Vorkarol. Min., plates 256b and 255b.

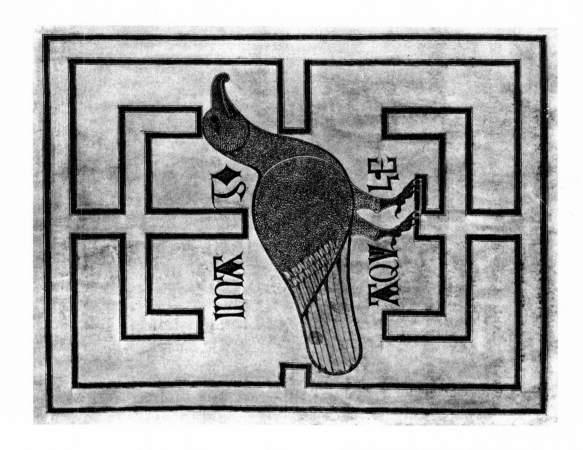

4

TRÈVES, CATHEDRAL TREASURY. 61 (134), (25,2 x 30,5 cm)

GOSPELS FROM THE LEGACY OF COUNT KESSELSTADT

Executed in Echternach or in the neighbouring Trèves about 775, partly on the basis of the Echternach Gospels (Paris, lat. 9389, cf. plate 3) and partly after Byzantine models. Continental uncial writing. Fol. 5ᵛ: « Thomas scribsit » (see plate 6).

FOL. 1ᵛ: THE SYMBOLS OF THE FOUR EVANGELISTS, IN THE MIDDLE BUST OF CHRIST (21 x 25,2 cm)

In the figures are russet, light and dark yellow tints, pink (flesh-tints, small parts of eagle) two tones of blue, purple in two gradations.
The frame is light yellow and Pompeii red (cf. ZIMMERMANN).

BIBLIOGRAPHY

ADA-HS., p. 104.
BRAUN, p. 65 ff.; ibid. further bibliography.
ZIMMERMANN, *Vorkarol. Min.*, p. 126, 281. Plates 258d and e, 267-279.

5

TRÈVES, CATHEDRAL TREASURY. 61 (134)

SEE PLATE 4

A. CANON-TABLE WITH THE BUST OF APOSTLE PETRUS

B. CANON-TABLE WITH BUST OF APOSTLE THOMAS

The figures in the canon-tables with blue drapery, grey cloak and yellow haloes on a blue ground. In the arcades several gradations of a yellow tint, two tones of green, two of blue, purple and brown, in the animals much grey and pink, (cf. ZIMMERMANN).

BIBLIOGRAPHY: *See plate 4.*

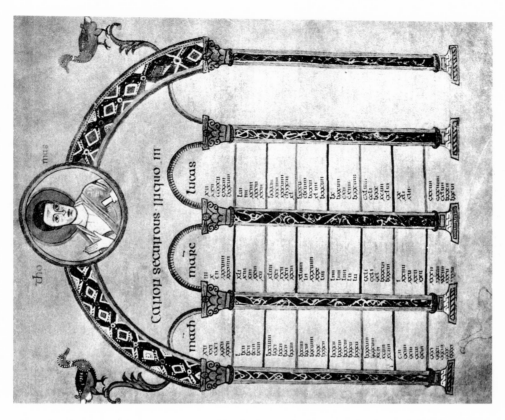

6

FOL. 51: THE TETRAMORPH. Artist Thomas (underneath signature: *Thomas scribsit*).

Colours: The drapery of the angel is blue, the cloak golden brown. The legs of the remaining symbols are in yellow and various brown tints. Flesh-tints are brownish, red outline and black interior lines. Hair is grey blue. Frame is light yellow and scarlet-vermilion. (cf. ZIMMERMANN).

BIBLIOGRAPHY: *See plate 4.*

mat
the
us.
euang̅
mar
cus.
euang̅

lu
cas.
euang̅
ioh
an
nis.
euang̅

thomas scribsit.

7

TRÈVES, CATHEDRAL TREASURY. 61 (134)

SEE PLATE 4

FOL. 9: TWO ARCHANGELS HOLD THE TITLE TABLET FOR THE GOSPEL OF ST. MATTHEW

After a Byzantine model. Background is pigeon blue and grey. Band for inscription left uncoloured. Undergarments light blue, cloaks are russet, relieved with white and drawn in brown. The wings are dark brown and brownish pink. Haloes and sceptre are yellow. Inscription tablet, base, frame royal blue, light yellow, brown and red. Flesh-tints pink, slightly working up to brownish. (cf. ZIMMERMANN).

BIBLIOGRAPHY: *See plate 4.*

8

See Plate 4

A. FOL. 6:   N(OVUM OPUS) 8,9 cm.

B. FOL. 183: V(ENIT) 3 cm.

C. FOL. 165: P(OST) 7,5 cm.

In N the animals are in light yellow on a black background. The initials in the shape of P and V principally in flat yellow and violet tints, red and green (cf. ZIMMERMANN).

BIBLIOGRAPHY: *See plate 4.*

9

TRÈVES, STADTBIBLIOTHEK. Cod. 23 (26,6 x 30,5 cm)

GOSPELS FROM STA. MARIA AD MARTYRES IN TRÈVES

Trèves? ninth century

VOL. II, FOL. 62: TITLEPAGE OF ST. JOHN

The faces painted over with silver, partly turned black. Drawing of features of Christ and the angel according to the Byzantine convention of colours: eyebrows and upper eyelid in brown, line between brow and lid red, lower eyelids in blue tint. For the rest, vermilion, chrome yellow, green, blue, light brown violet.

BIBLIOGRAPHY

BEISSEL, *Evang. Bch.*, p. 157 f.
BRAUN, p. 76 f.; ibid. further bibliographical references.
HASELOFF, *Egb. Psalter*, p. 213 (addition to p. 147).

photo Rheinisches Museum, Cologne

INITI
VM SCI
EVVANGELII
SECVNDV
IOHANNE

10

TRÈVES, STADTBIBLIOTHEK. COD. 23

SEE PLATE 9

VOL. II, FOL. 63: BEGINNING OF THE GOSPEL OF ST. JOHN
For colour see plate 9.

BIBLIOGRAPHY: *See plate 9.*

photo Rheinisches Museum, Cologne

PRIN
CIPIO

ERAT
VERBVₘ

II

A. ST. GALL, STIFTSBIBLIOTHEK. COD. 1395

SINGLE LEAVES

Irish (or written by an Irish scribe in Switzerland), towards the middle of 8th century.

PAG. 422: ORNAMENTED PAGE IN FOUR COMPARTMENTS (15,4 x 20,5 cm)
Colours: orange, chrome yellow, cadmium yellow, lilac, violet. The ornaments of the connecting bars and the border left white on a black ground. The ground of the middle-piece is also black (cf. ZIMMERMANN).

BIBLIOGRAPHY

ZIMMERMANN, *Vorkarol. Min.*, p. 243; plate 197a; ibid. further bibliographical references.

B. MUNICH, STAATSBIBLIOTHEK. COD. LAT. 19101
(27 x 42 cm)

GOSPELS FROM TEGERNSEE

where they were as early as 980; ninth century, executed probably in Trèves and no doubt brought to Tegernsee by the abbot Hartwich of Tegernsee who had come thither from St. Maximin (978-82).

FOL. 16^v: ORNAMENTED PAGE IN FOUR COMPARTMENTS
Colours: minium, green and gold tints.

BIBLIOGRAPHY

BANGE, *Malerschule*, p. 4.
CHROUST, Series II, No. 1, plate 4, where also further bibliographical references.

12

VIENNA, NATIONALBIBLIOTHEK. Cod. 1007 (Salisb. 181)
(17,2 x 26 cm)
St. John Chrysostomus

Homeliae in Mathaeum, beginning of ninth century. Written in Salzburg and painted under the influence of insular models.

FOL. 1: St. John Chrysostomus

The ground is in vellum colour, pale green in the lunette. Undergarment is green with red stripes.
Paenula is red with blue border; black, light red and yellow tints in interior lines. Halo yellow with blue outline. Flesh-tint light pink, with brown and red drawing. For the rest, pale green, blue, minium, and vellum coloured tints. (cf. HERMANN).

BIBLIOGRAPHY

Hermann, I, p. 141, ibid. further bibliographical references.
Swarzenski II, p. 8 ff.

13

VIENNA, NATIONALBIBLIOTHEK. Cod. 387 (25,2 x 32 cm)

COMPUTISTIC-ASTRONOMICAL COLLECTIVE WORK

Written in Salzburg between 809 and 821 (probably 818) after a north French model, cf. plate 14.

FOL. 90ᵛ: REPRESENTATION OF MONTHS

Flat colours: brown, chamois, minium, green, grey and green, grey and blue, blue, brown drawing. Flesh-tint drawn in pink and brown.

BIBLIOGRAPHY

CHROUST, Series I, number 1, plate 1.
HERMANN, p. 145 ff., ibid. further bibliographical references.
SWARZENSKI, I, p. 19, note 2.
SWARZENSKI, II, p. 17 ff.

14

MUNICH, STAATSBIBLIOTHEK. Cod. lat. 210 (23,9 x 32,5 cm)
COMPUTISTIC-ASTRONOMICAL COMPILATION

Salzburg, 818. Preserved in the monastery of St. Emmeram since the end of
the tenth century. To judge from entries it seems to have been in Salzburg
in the ninth century, where there was another similar Ms.: Vienna 387 (see
plate 13). Clm. 210 was also probably copied from the same model. The latter,
to judge from its martyrology, seems to have originated in the North-West
of the Frankish Kingdom.
An indication of particular significance is the entry of St. Amand in whose
monastery Arn of Salzburg was abbot. He may well have brought the
model with him to Salzburg. Cf. plate 80.

FOL. 113^v: CELESTIAL MAP

*Painted brown upon a green coloured vellum, little black (outlines in the shades,
white contour lines, external circles minium).*

BIBLIOGRAPHY

CHROUST, Series I, number 1, plate 1 and 2.
HASELOFF, *Malerschule*, p. 73 f.
HERMANN, p. 146.
SWARZENSKI, I, p. 12, 19, note 2.
SWARZENSKI, II, p. 13 ff.

15

MUNICH, STAATSBIBLIOTHEK. COD. LAT. 210

SEE PLATE 14

FOL. 117ᵛ: CONSTELLATION OF AURIGA AND TAURUS

Only red and green tints are employed, although in several gradations. The bull consists of a contour drawing in minium, washed over with a dirty greyish green tint. Ground in a green tint.

BIBLIOGRAPHY: *See plate 14.*

Inposteriori genui.
Inpropoda claream unam
summa XVIII. Videntur
& aliae iuxta caudam eius
stellę obscurae VIII.

singulas. Insummitate
manus duas. Insinistra
menu duas qui uocantur
hcedi. summa.
VIIII

Auriga uel agitator queme
ricthonium dicunt. habet
stellam incapite I. Insingulis
umeris singulas. Insinistro
claeorem quae appellatur
capra. Insingulis genibus

Taurus habet stellas in utro
q; cornu I. In utroque
oculo I. In naso I. hae quin
q; hyades appellentur.
In ungula III. In collo II.
In dorso II. ultimam clayo
rem. subuentre unam.
In pectore unam claram
summa XV sunt & sep
te stellę quaath
lentiderū piadas
uocant. quarum sex
uidentur sep ma obscura
est dicuntur que incauda
tauri positae.

16

ROME, VATICANA. Pal. lat. 1564

De Agrimensoria

From Fulda, where the Codex is known to have existed in the 16th century. Anyhow a product of the Fulda School, towards the middle of the ninth century.

A. Fol. 1: Miniature of the imperator *(round picture)*

Inscription *(17th century)*: «*Imperatoris tamquam Agrimensoriae supremi judicis ac principis effigies*». Below there is another bust not named. Cloak of emperor in red, armour in yellow, hair brown, ground blue, frame a sorrel tint (cf. Zimmermann).

B. Fol. 3: Gathering of authors

Inscription *(17th century)*: «*Idem qui proximus superior consilii judiciique de finibus et controversiis agrorum typus. Praeses*».

BIBLIOGRAPHY

Beissel, *Vat. Min.*, plate II, p. 3 f.
Clemen, *Fulda*, p. 123.
Zimmermann, *Fulda*, p. 90 ff., plate 12.

17

ROME, VATICANA. Vat. lat. 3868 (28,8 x 34,1 cm)

Terentii opera

From Corvey. Painted by the monk Adelricus of Corvey under abbot Adelardus (822-826) in whose company he came from Corbie when Nova Corbeia was founded. It is questionable, therefore, whether the MS. was brought from Corbie or was written at Corvey. The first assumption is the more likely one. The scribe calls himself Rhodgarius; a monk of this name is mentioned at Corvey under abbot Warinus (826-856).

Fol. 2: Portrait of Terentius

Colours: The tints employed in the miniatures of the Codex are white, white-grey, dark blue, yellow, red, green and dark brown (cf. BETHE).

BIBLIOGRAPHY

BEISSEL, *Vat. Min.* III. B., p. 6 f.

BETHE, Sp. 8-11, Plate IIa, III, IV.

C. R. MOREY, *I Miniatori del Terenzio illustrato della Bibl. Vat.* - Rendiconti della Pontificia Accademia Romana di Archeologia IV, 1926, p. 27.

TERENTI

18

A. ROME, VATICANA. Vat. lat. 3868

See plate 17

Scene from Andria I, 1, v. 28: Simo calls the cook Sosias and sends the others into the house.

For colours and literature, see plate 17

B. PARIS, BIBLIOTHÈQUE NATIONALE. Cod. lat. 7899
(20 x 25,5 cm)

Terentius from St. Denis

France, ninth century. The same scene as in A. Pen drawing in the colour of the writing, in some places shaded over by the brush.

BIBLIOGRAPHY

Bethe, Sp. 11 ff., ibid. further bibliography and numerous reproductions.

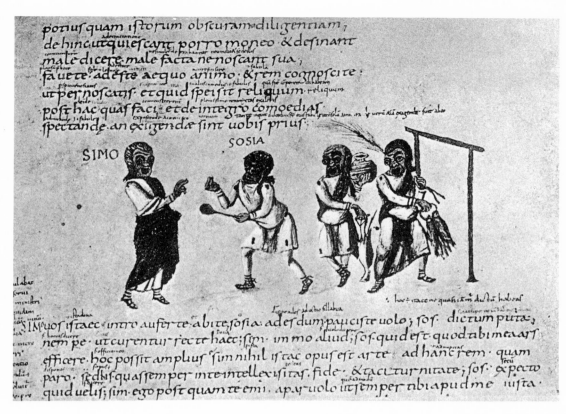

potiuf quam iftorum obfcuram diligentiam;
de hinc utquiefcant. porro moneo & definant
male dicere. male facta ne nofcant fua;
fauete. adefte aequo animo. & rem cognofcite;
ut pernofcatif. etquid fperfit reliquum.
poft hac quaf faci. etde integro comoediaf.
fpectande. an exigende fint uobif priuf;

SIMO   SOSIA

SIM. uof iftaec intro auferte. abite fofia; adef dum. paucif te uolo; fof. dictum puta;
nem pe. ut curentur recte haec; fim. immo aliud; fof. quid eft quod tibi mea arf.
efficere hoc pofsit amplius. fim nihil iftaec opuf eft arte. ad hanc rem. quam
paro. fed if quaf femper in te intellexi fitaf. fide. & taciturnitate; fof. expecto.
quid uelif; fim. ego poft quam te emi. a paruolo ut femper tibi apud me iufta.

Male dicere malefacta penofcant fua
Fauete. adeftre arquo animo. & rem cognofcite
U fperriofcatif. & quid fperfit relicuum
P oft hac. quaf faciet deintegro comoediuf
S pectunde. an exigendae fint uobif priuf

SIMO   SOSIA

Symo   Sosia

V of eftaee intro auferte; abire fofia;
A def dum; paucif te uolo; fof; dictum puta;
N em pe. ut curentur recte haec. immo aliud   quideft
Q uod tibi mea arf efficere hocpofsit amplius
N ihiliftaec opuf eft arte. ad hanc rem quam paro

19

CASSEL, LANDESBIBLIOTHEK. Ms. Phys. fol. 10 (21 x 28 cm)

Herbaria of Apulejus and Antonius Musa

Tenth century. Possibly written in Fulda, where the MS. was preserved for a long time. It is closely connected with the older MS. at Leyden, Voss. Qu. 9. (seventh century) which is probably of Lower Italian origin.

A. The enthroned Aesculapius. *Inscription:* (AE)SCOLAPIUS MEDICUS MAG(ISTER). *On the scroll:* MEDICINA.

The colours are somewhat dirty. Tunic in light grey, blue with brown shades, the lights are laid on in a white tint. Cloak tawny, shaded in deep brown. Clavi and hem of cloak are red. The scroll is in dark purple with white letters. Tints of the flesh heavy red, with black in the shades and white in the lights. Hair and beard are in brown and black. The circles from top to bottom contain the following tints: green with yellow and red lines and yellow writing; red with yellow circumference and grey plants; green with red and grey borders, the plants are in black, red and yellow.

B. Fol. 27: Two plants (Salvia and Coliandrum).

BIBLIOGRAPHY

Charles Singer, *The Herbal in Antiquity* etc. in: *The Journal of Hellenic Studies,* Vol. 47, 1927. Part I, p. 43 ff.

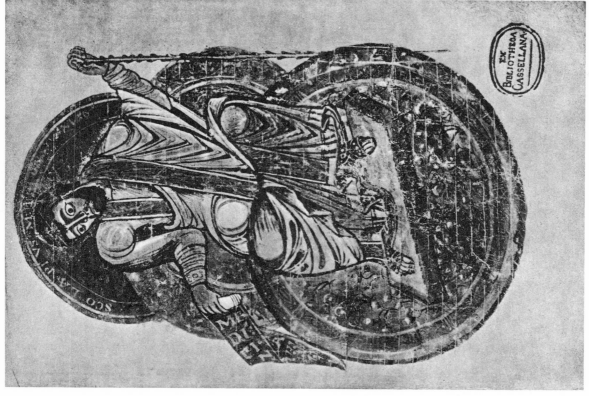

20

Fol. I^v/2: Two disputing authors

Fol. I^v/2: Two disputing authors

The one to the left is designated on a later inscription as Constantinus Mag-(ister), the lower portion of the one to the right is torn off. A headgear similar to that of the figure to the left is also worn by the physicians Gallienus and Hippocrates as late as the 13th century in the frescoes of the crypt at Anagni. A famous physician of Salerno in the eleventh century was called Constantinus, but the manuscript can scarcely be assigned to so late a date; it is probably a question of a later interpretation. The MS. contains also the pictures of the authors « Ypocras » and « Apollo ».

Colours: Left: the background is in dark green, the tunic yellow with brown in the shades and red in the edge. The cap and the steps of the throne are also yellow. Cloak bluish black with grey in the lights. The curtains are in brown and red with black in the shades. The roof, cushions, and book are also in red tints. Tints of the flesh as in plate 19. Right: Tunic in red brown, cloak in green with yellow in the lights and black in the shades; the under sleeves are yellow, the book green with a yellow edge; the spire is violet. Lower curtain is in dark blue with black in the shades and white in the lights. Hair brown.

BIBLIOGRAPHY: *See plate 19.*

21

VIENNA, SCHATZKAMMER
Purple Gospels with Golden Letters

Aix-la-Chapelle (?) beginning of the ninth century. On the first page of the Gospel of St. Luke, the margin exhibits in golden rustic capitals the following inscription: DEMETRIUS PRESBYTER.

Fol. 15: The Evangelist Matthew

Drapery and book are in a white tint with grey in the shades. The landscape background is in deep brown tones working up to a grey tint, the sky is pale bluish grey; the acanthus border is dull grey. The cushions are in a brilliant minium red tint; the flesh is russet. Hair black and brown. Much gold is used in halo, chair, desk, writing utensils and frame bar.

BIBLIOGRAPHY

Ada-Hs., p. 72 f., plates 20-22.
Arneth, coloured plates.
Boinet, plates 58 and 59.
W. Köhler, *Ber. d. dtsch. Ver. f. Kw.* 1911, p. 80.
L. von Schlosser, *Die Schatzkammer in Wien,* Vienna, 1918, p. 36 ff. plates I and II.
Swarzenski I, p. 7, 17 note 24.
Swarzenski, *Reims,* p. 84 ff.

22

VIENNA, SCHATZKAMMER
GOSPELS, *See plate 21.*

FOL. 178ᵛ: THE EVANGELIST JOHN

Architecture and footstool are in dark brown with golden details. Otherwise, like the St. Matthew, plate 21.

BIBLIOGRAPHY: *See plate 21.*

23

AIX-LA-CHAPELLE, CATHEDRAL TREASURY
GOSPELS (21,7 x 30 cm)

Aix-la-Chapelle? Beginning of the ninth century.

FOL. 13: THE FOUR EVANGELISTS

Colours: the hills are in blue and green tints, the Evangelists in white garments with blue haloes. Cushions are red. The frame is gold with blue gems between blue borders (cf. BEISSEL).

BIBLIOGRAPHY

ADA-HS., p. 74.
ST. BEISSEL, *Das Karolingische Evangelienbuch d. Aachener Münsters* in *Zeitschr. f. christl. Kst.*, 1888, p. 53 ff.
BOINET, pl. 60a.
FRIEND, *Arch. Congr. Ithaca*, 1926.
SWARZENSKI, *Reims*, p. 85 f.

photo Mertens, Aix-la-Chapelle

24

BERLIN, STAATSBIBLIOTHEK. THEOL. LAT. FOL. 260
(24 x 32,5 cm)
GOSPELS FROM CLEVES

Aix-la-Chapelle? Beginning of ninth century.

FOL. 75ᵛ: THE EVANGELIST MARK

Drapery and scroll are white with tawny and sea green shades. Background behind the Evangelists is in deep sea green; for the rest, tawny and sea green and yellow tones are used. The sky is in white working up to a yellowish grey. The symbol is brown, tawny and greyish yellow. The desk and inner frame edge are in a light and dark sea green tint. Cushions, writing and pen are in glaring red. Flesh brownish working up to a bluish tint. The same tone is also employed in the inkhorn, footstool and throne. Frame, halo, and parts of throne are in gold.

BIBLIOGRAPHY

BOINET, Plate 70.
SWARZENSKI, *Reims*, p. 87.
SWARZENSKI, II, p. 28 note 2.

25

PARIS, BIBLIOTHÈQUE NATIONALE. Nouv. Acq. 1203
Purple-Gospels from St. Sernin at Toulouse

Written by Godescalc for Charlemagne, cf. the dedicatory poem (Dümmler, *Poetae lat.*, I, 95). The writing of Godescalc is considered to be identical with hand I of the Ada Hs. About 781.

FOL. 3: ENTHRONED CHRIST

Tunic in bluish black, cloak in a brownish violet. The lines of the features follow the Byzantine convention, the contours of hands and feet are red in the lights and black in the shades.

BIBLIOGRAPHY

ADA-HS., p. 1 f., 85 f., plate 25.
BEISSEL, *Evang. Bch.*, p. 164 ff.
BOINET, pl. 3-4.
GOLDSCHMIDT, p. 6 f., 9 f., 21.
HASELOFF, *Egb. Psalter*, p. 166.
HERMANN, p. 57.
KÖHLER, *Adagruppe*, p. 257 f.
STRZYGOWSKI, p. 58 ff.
SWARZENSKI, I, p. 6, 16 note 9, 42 note, 91 note.

26

PARIS, BIBLIOTHÈQUE NATIONALE. Nouv. Acq. 1203

See plate 25

Fol. 1ᵛ: The Evangelist Mark

Dirty colours. The background from bottom to top is greenish, light bluish, dark blue with gold letters, light pink. The tunic is violet, the cloak dark blue, cushions are minium, haloes and footstool are gilt. Black outlines, lights laid on in white. Flesh orange, the modelling slightly greenish, the drawing of the faces according to Byzantine convention of colours. The frame is blue, purple and minium.

BIBLIOGRAPHY: *See plate 25.*

27

PARIS, BIBLIOTHÈQUE NATIONALE. Nouv. Acq. 1203

See plate 25

The Evangelist Luke. *The colours are similar to those on Plate 25.*

Bibliography: *See plate 25.*

28

PARIS, BIBLIOTHÈQUE NATIONALE. Nouv. Acq. 1203

SEE PLATE 25

FOL. 3^v: FOUNTAIN OF LIFE

BIBLIOGRAPHY: *See plate 25.*

29

TRÈVES, STADTBIBLIOTHEK. N. 22 (24,5 x 36,5 cm)

Ada-Ms. (Gospels)

From St. Maximin at Trèves, where it can be proved to have been as early as the 12th century. Dedicatory verses:

QVEM DEVOTA DEO JVSSIT PERSCRIBERE MATER
ADA ANCILA DEI, PVLCHRISQVE ORNARE METALLIS.

(For the personality of Ada, see Ada-Hs. p. 10 ff.). Ada group, 8th to 9th century.

Fol. 15ᵛ: The Evangelist Matthew

The tunic is in vigorous blue, the cloak is yellow and brown with a minium red canopy, the architecture is bright carmine; lunette ground is carmine, the columns are green, the bases and capitals are minium red, the haloes are either golden or alternately silver and gold, otherwise little gold is used. The flesh is orange, mod-elled in grey and green relieved with white. The drawing of the faces is accord-ing to the Byzantine convention of colours. Hands and feet are as on plate 25.

BIBLIOGRAPHY

Ada-Hs.
Boinet, pl. 7b and 8.
Goldschmidt, I, p. 5 ff., ibid. further bibliography.
Haseloff, *Egb. Psalter*, p. 47, 58 ff., 87, 126, 165 ff.
Swarzenski, I, p. 5 ff.

30

PARIS, BIBLIOTHÈQUE DE L'ARSENAL. Cod. 599
(19 x 26,5 cm)

GOSPELS

According to a later entry from St. Martin-des-Champs in Paris. Ada group. Beginning of the ninth century.

FOL. 61: INITIAL PAGE OF THE GOSPEL OF ST. MARK

Letters and ornamentations are in gold, silver and a little minium on a purple ground. Frame left white with gold ornaments. The frame edge is in silver and gold.

BIBLIOGRAPHY

ADA-HS., p. 86.
BASTARD, pl. 88-90.
BOINET, pl. 11.
HASELOFF, *Egb. Psalter*, p. 164.
H. MARTIN, *Catalogue des Manuscrits de la Bibl. de l'Arsenal*, I, 451, Paris, 1885.

photo Deutscher Verein f. Kunstw.

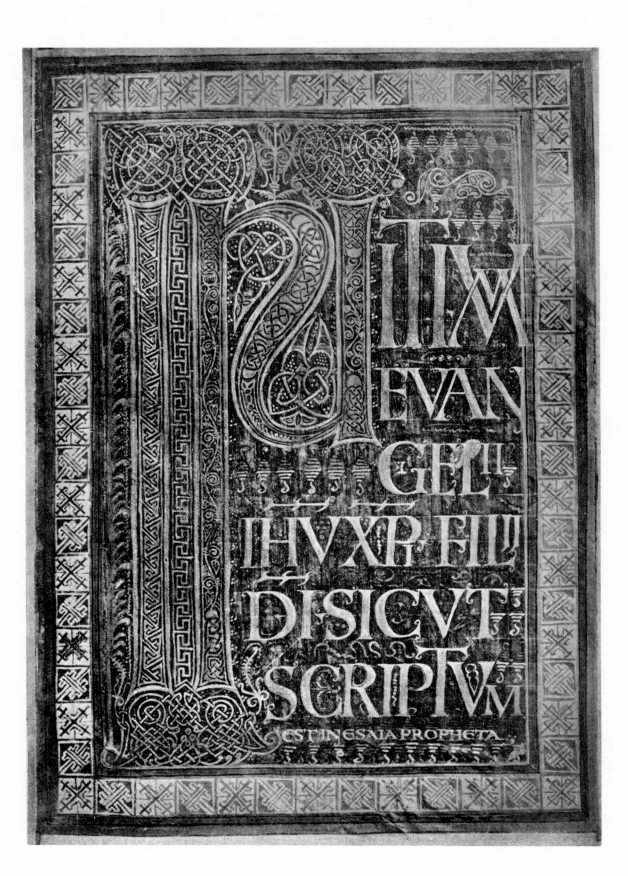

31

PARIS, BIBLIOTHÈQUE NATIONALE. Cod. lat. 8850
(26 x 36 cm)
GOSPELS FROM ST. MÉDARD IN SOISSONS

According to a tradition of the monastery, the manuscript was made a present to St. Médard in 827 under Louis the Pious and the Empress Judith. Ada group, beginning of the ninth century.

FOL. 7: CANON-TABLE

BIBLIOGRAPHY

ADA-Hs., p. 9, 89 ff., Plates 31-34.
BASTARD, pl. 91 ff.
BEISSEL, *Evang. Bch.,* p. 177 f.
BOINET, plates 18-23.
FLEURY, *Les Manuscrits à Miniatures de la Bibl. de Soissons.,* pp. 3-47.
GOLDSCHMIDT, I, p. 10.
HASELOFF, *Egb. Psalter,* pp. 112, 126 ff., 131 ff., 135, 165, 167.
STRZYGOWSKI, p. 61.

photo Deutscher Verien f. Kunstw.

32

Fol. 1: Title page with the lamb and the twenty-four elders

The stripes of ground are in violet and brown working up to a bright lilac. Architecture is pale blue with white. The background above has two stripes, shaded in violet and brown working up to a light lilac, and one stripe in blue. The Medallions are blue, and the architecture is in tints between yellow and brown. The curtain is minium with gold drawing. The columns are in deep green and lilac-brown. In the details the same colours, particularly minium are employed.

BIBLIOGRAPHY: *See plate* 31.

photo Deutscher Verein f. Kunstw.

33

PARIS, BIBLIOTHÈQUE NATIONALE. Cod. lat. 8850
See plate 31

Fol. 180ᵛ: The Evangelist John. On the book the text of John III, 36.

Bibliography: *See plate* 31.

photo Deutscher Verein f. Kunstw.

34

FOL. 6ᵛ: FOUNTAIN OF LIFE

The soil is bistre. Architecture below is green, above lilac with yellow stripes finishing in yellow. The sky is dark slate blue working up to bright blue and white. Architecture of fountain is blue, lilac, minium, light and dark grey with a good deal of gold and silver. The water is blue. In the frame the same tints are employed. The big animals are in brown, pale blue, grey and yellow.

BIBLIOGRAPHY: *See plate 31.*

photo Deutscher Verein f. Kunstw.

35

LONDON, BRITISH MUSEUM. Harley 2788 (25 x 37 cm)

Gospels

Bought by Harley in the Hague from J. J. Charron in 1720. Ada group, about 800.

Fol. 11ᵛ: Canon-table

The small figures on the columns are in white on a blue ground.

BIBLIOGRAPHY

Ada-Hs., p. 9, 86 f.
Boinet, pl. 12-14.
Haseloff, *Egb. Psalter*, p. 112, 126.
Herbert, p. 100, plate 9.
Warner, pl. 4-5.

photo Deutscher Verein f. Kunstw.

36

LONDON, BRITISH MUSEUM. HARLEY 2788

SEE PLATE 35

FOL. 13ᵛ: THE EVANGELIST MATTHEW. On the book the text of Matth. XI, 28.

Colours: The tunic is light blue with minium lining, the cloak is violet, the cushion minium with light blue stripes, the canopy of the throne is dark green. The curtains are minium with blue lining. The footstool and the greatest part of the throne are yellowish. The architecture has blue stripes, the tympanum of the arch is violet. The lower part of background is sea-green. The same colours are used in the details, with the addition of English red. The frame, rays of halo etc. are golden.

BIBLIOGRAPHY: *See plate 35.*

photo Deutscher Verein f. Kunstw.

37

LONDON, BRITISH MUSEUM. HARLEY 2788

SEE PLATE 35

FOL. 161ᵛ: THE EVANGELIST JOHN

The tunic is golden with red strokes, the cloak is purple and gold. The canopy is dark green, the background is vermilion. The lights have been blackened in many places.

BIBLIOGRAPHY: *See plate 35.*

photo Deutscher Verein f. Kunstw.

38

KARLSBURG (GYULAFEHÉRVÁR), ROUMANIA
BATTHYÁNEUM

GOSPELS OF ST. MATTHEW AND MARK (26,8 x 36,7 cm)

The Codex, the second half of which is preserved in the Vaticana (Pal. lat. 50), comes from St. Nazarius at Lorsch and must evidently be identified with the Evangeliarium « pictum cum auro scriptum habens tabulas ebur-neas » of the oldest Catal. of the library of Lorsch (ninth century, Becker, *Catal. bibl. ant.* No. 37). Ada group, beginning of the ninth century.

PAGE 24: CANON-TABLE.

BIBLIOGRAPHY

GOLDSCHMIDT, I, p. 13.
HERMANN, p. 58.
KOEHLER, *Adagruppe,* p. 259 ff.
SCHMIDT, p. 51 ff.
R. SZENTIVÁNY, *Der Codex Aureus von Lorsch, jetzt in Gyulafehérvár-Studien u. Mitt. z. Gesch. d. Bened. Ordens,* N. F. 2 (1912), p. 131-151.

photo Deutscher Verein f. Kunstw.

39

KARLSBURG (GYULAFEHÉRVÁR), ROUMANIA
BATTHYÁNEUM

Gospels from Lorsch

See plate 38

Pag. 36: Maiestas Domini

Purple ground with golden lettering; inner compartment of the circle is blue. The tunic is blue with white lights and black lines of shade, the cloak is brownish. Hair brown, throne and halo are golden.

BIBLIOGRAPHY: *See plate 38.*

photo Deutscher Verein f. Kunstw.

40

KARLSBURG (GYULAFEHÉRVÁR), ROUMANIA
BATTHYÁNEUM

GOSPELS FROM LORSCH

SEE PLATE 38

PAG. 26: THE EVANGELIST MATTHEW

The tunic is blue with white in the lights; the cloak is red with golden lights; the hills are lilac with green and lilac coloured plants. The wings of the angel are red, the columns darkly grained.

BIBLIOGRAPHY: *See plate 38.*

photo Deutscher Verein f. Kunstw.

41

KARLSBURG (GYULAFEHÉRVÁR), ROUMANIA
BATTHYÁNEUM

Gospels from Lorsch

See plate 38

Pag. 37: Ornamented page ⸱ Liber generationis
Particularly gold and silver forms upon a purple ground are employed.

Bibliography: *See plate 38.*

photo Deutscher Verein f. Kunstw.

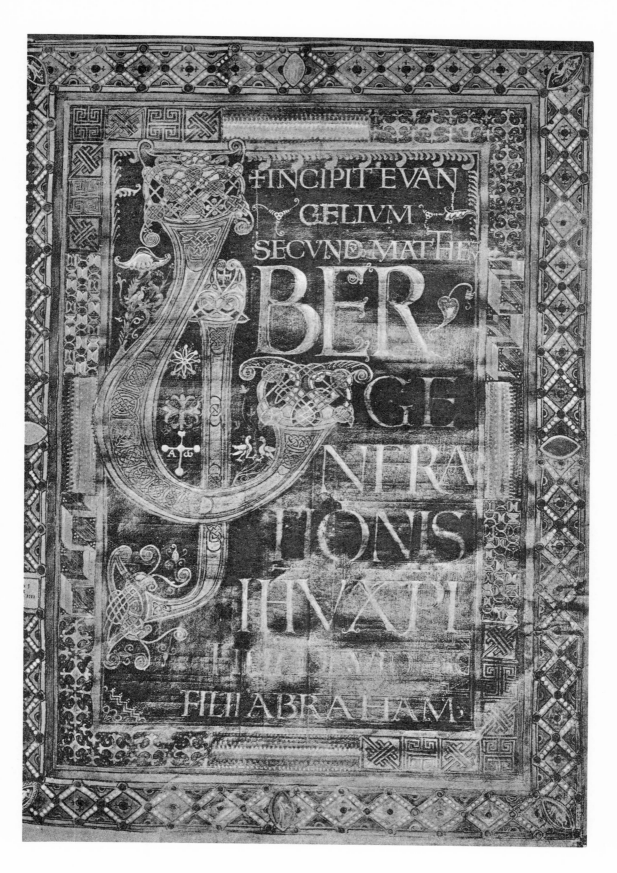

✝INCIPIT·EVAN
GELIVM
SECVNDMATHEV
LIBER·
GE
NERA
TIONIS
IHV·XPI
FILII·ABRAHAM.

42

ABBEVILLE, BIBLIOTHÈQUE MUNICIPALE
Cod. 4 (1) (25 x 35 cm)
Purple Gospels

The Manuscript is alleged to have been a gift from Charlemagne to Abbot Angilbert (790-814) of St. Ricquier. It is mentioned in 831 in the inventory of the treasury of St. Ricquier. Ada group, about 800.

Fol. 17ᵛ: The Evangelist Matthew

The tunic is blue with white in the lights, the cloak is purple relieved with gold. The flesh is laid on in green, relieved with yellowish white and pink.

BIBLIOGRAPHY

Alcius Ledieu, *Catalogue analytique des Mss. de la Bibl. d'Abbeville*, 1885, p. 3 ff.

Ada-Hs., p. 87 f.

Boinet, pl. 7a, 9, 10.

Haseloff, *Egb. Psalter*, pp. 126, 165, 167.

photo Kunstgesch. Seminar, Marburg

43

ABBEVILLE, BIBLIOTHÈQUE MUNICIPALE. Cod. 4 (1)

SEE PLATE 42

FOL. 66: THE EVANGELIST MARK

Colours are very much scaled off. The background is green, in the lunette lazu-lite blue. The carpet above the arm of throne is light brown; the undergarment in pale blue; the cloak in darker blue, the cushion in red; the columns are blue and white. Golden haloes (cf. LEDIEU).

BIBLIOGRAPHY: *See plate 42.*

photo Kunstgesch. Seminar, Marburg

INITIVM
EVANGELII
IHV XPI
FILII DI

STRIPTU
EST IN
ESAIA
PROPHE:

AICVT

44

FOL. 102: INITIAL Q(UONIAM) TO ST. LUKE

The nearly illegible inscriptions of the names in the roundels are to be interpreted «Zacharias» and «Angelus Dei» (Annunciation to Zachariah). Purple ground. Initials and plaitwork are in gold and minium. The heads are on a light blue ground, the columns (very much worn off) are in blue with golden, white ornamented bands. The acanthus pattern of the arch is minium. The birds and tendrils are white.

BIBLIOGRAPHY: *See plate 42.*

photo Kunstgesch. Seminar, Marburg

INCIPIT
ANGELIVM·SEC·D
LV CAM
NIAM
QVIDEM
MVLTI
CONATI·SVN

45

PARIS, BIBLIOTHÈQUE NATIONALE. Cod. lat. 8849
(28 x 39 cm)
GOSPELS FROM THE CATHEDRAL TREASURY OF METZ

where they are mentioned in 1775. Ada group, ninth century.

FOL. 18ᵛ: THE EVANGELIST MATTHEW

The tunic is chrome yellow with green shades, the cloak is slate blue, with yellow in the lights. The flesh-tones are pink. Black outlines and folds. The background between the columns is parchment coloured, in the lunette it is in variegated stripes with gold stars.

BIBLIOGRAPHY

BASTARD, pl. 105.
SWARZENSKI, I, p. 17 note 17.
WEBER, pl. 32-38.

photo Deutscher Verein f. Kunstw.

46

GOTHA, LANDESBIBLIOTHEK. Cod. I, 21. (21,5 x 33 cm)

GOSPELS FROM ST. MARTIN IN MAINZ

Entry of Mainz of 1479. The initials are closely connected with insular art, St. Luke and St. Mark are perhaps following an insular model. Ada group, beginning of the ninth century.

FOL. 80: THE EVANGELIST LUKE

The background is green with minium stripes in the borders. The cloak is minium with minium and black drawing. The cushions are violet with brown stripes and white, yellow and red dots. The symbol is brown and tawny with a little violet. The legend is yellow and red. The same colours are used in the remaining portions of the plate. The flesh-colour is similar to that of plate 47, but laid on more thinly.

BIBLIOGRAPHY

BEISSEL, *Evang. Bch.*, p. 182 note 3.

DOERING and VOSS, p. 88, pl. 101.

FRZ. JACOBS and F. A. Uckert, *Beiträge zur älteren Lit. oder Merkw. d. brzgl. öffentl. Bibl. zu Gotha*, II, p. 36, N. 40, Leipzig 1836.

SWARZENSKI, I, p. 7, 17 note, 18, 115 note.

photo Deutscher Verein f. Kunstw.

47

FOL. 125ᵛ: THE EVANGELIST JOHN

The background is green, exhibiting in the lunette a brown and violet patterned stripe. The drapery is tawny, drawn in green and minium. The lining is green and yellow. The cloak and cushions are minium with darker minium coloured and white strokes. The throne-hangings are thinly drawn in dark lilac, grey and light lilac colours. The symbol is light brown. The legend is in green and yellow colours, and the haloes are yellow. The shafts of the columns are green and yellow; the tympanum of the arcades is violet and red and whitish yellow. The same colours are also used in the remaining portions of the plate. The flesh-colour is pink grey with green shades. In the drawing of the features the Byzantine convention of colours is followed.

BIBLIOGRAPHY: *See plate 46.*

photo Deutscher Verein f. Kunstw.

48

GOTHA, LANDESBIBLIOTHEK. COD. I. 21
SEE PLATE 46

FOL. 126: INITIAL I(N PRINCIPIO) TO ST. JOHN

The drawing and the ground of the trunk are in black and brown colours. The animals and the plaitwork are green, minium yellow, and (rarely) violet thinly laid on. The accompanying rows of dots are in minium.

BIBLIOGRAPHY: *See plate 46.*

photo Deutscher Verein f. Kunstw.

+ INCPT EVAN
GELVMSECVN
DVM IONNEM

NPRN
CIPIO
ERAT
VERBV
ETVER
BVM
ERAT
APVD
DMLHIDS

erat bum. hoc erat in prin
cipio apud dm omnia per
ipsum facta sunt & sine
ipso factum est nihil.
Quod factum est in ipso
uita est & uita erat
lux hominum & lux in
tenebris lucet. & tene
bre eam non con prae
henderunt. Fuit homo
missus a do cui nomen erat
Iohannes. hic
uenit in testimonium ut
testimonium per hibert
de lumine. ut omnes p
illum crederent. Non
erat ille lux sed ut testi
monium per hiber & de
lumine. Erat lux uera
que inluminat omnem
hominem uenientem
in hunc mundum.
In hoc mundo erat &
mundus per ipsum fac
tus est & mundus eum
non cognouit. In sua
propria uenit & sui
eum non receperunt
Quot quot autem re
ceperunt eum dedit

49

COLOGNE, DOMBIBLIOTHEK. Cod. 14
Gospels

Cologne? ninth century. After a Franco-Saxon model.

A. Fol. 160ᵛ: The Evangelist John. Caption:

MORE VOLANS AQVILAE
VERBO PETIT ASTRA IOHANNES

Vellum ground, drapery dirty red, drawn with black, white and grey.

B. Fol. 161ᵛ: Initial IN (to St. John)

BIBLIOGRAPHY

Beissel, *Evang. Bch.,* p. 156 f., 334.
Boinet, pl. 108 d.
Ehl, p. 32 ff.

50

MUNICH, STAATSBIBLIOTHEK. Cod. lat. 17011 (21 x 18,5 cm)
Gospels from Schäftlarn

Executed by order of bishop Anno of Freising (854-875), closely allied to Munich Cod. lat. 6215.

A. Fol. 81ᵛ: The Evangelist Mark

The ground is purple, the drapery bright orange, modelled with bright purple and white. The flesh-tint is russet relieved with white. The outlines are mostly traced over afterwards in brown.

B. Fol. 116ᵛ: Q(uoniam quidem)

Dirty green with cadmium and gold; edged with brown lines.

BIBLIOGRAPHY

Ada-Hs., p. 104.
Bange, *Malerschule*, p. 15 note, 56.
Beissel, *Evang. Bch.*, p. 250, repr. 75-76.
Hermann, I, p. 135.
Swarzenski, I, p. 17 note 27.
Swarzenski, *Reims*, p. 93 f.

50 B: *photo Staatl. Bildstelle, Berlin.*

51

VIENNA, NATIONALBIBLIOTHEK. COD. 1234 (19,5 x 27,5 cm)

GOSPELS FROM WELTENBURG (NEAR KELHEIM)

Bavarian, middle or latter half of ninth century. Probably written at Weltenburg where the MS. existed as early as 926. Allied to Munich Cod. lat. 17011 (see plate 50) and Cod. 6215.

FOL. 14ᵛ: THE EVANGELIST ST. MATTHEW
Pen-drawing in brown.

BIBLIOGRAPHY

HERMANN, p. 134 ff., ibid. reprod. and further bibliographical reference. SWARZENSKI, *Reims,* p. 94.

52

INNSBRUCK, UNIVERSITÄTSBIBLIOTHEK. Cod. 484
(18 x 22,5 cm)

Gospels of the church at Innichen

Alamannic? Latter half of ninth century.

Fol. 110ᵛ: The Evangelist Luke. On the band text of Luk. I. 5.

Drapery and symbol are yellow, the cloak and cushion are red. The band containing text is purple with golden letters. For the rest, mainly red and green tints are used; the details are in gold and silver (cf. Hermann).

BIBLIOGRAPHY

Beissel, *Evang. Bch.,* p. 160, 251.

Hermann, Jul., *Die illuminierten Hss. in Tirol ⁄ Beschr. Vzchnis d. illum. Hss. in Österr. I. Tirol,* p. 201 ff., repr. 92⁄96.

Merton, p. 48 note 41.

Swarzenski II, p. 41 note 2.

53

MUNICH, STAATSBIBLIOTHEK. Cod. lat. 14345 (20 x 27,8 cm)

Pauli Epistolae

Further cycle of Ada group, possibly executed at Ratisbon, end of the ninth century.

Fol. 1ᵛ: Stoning of St. Stephen

The background is in a dirty green tint, the arcade is blue violet with minium and cadmium. The same tints are used in the drapery.

Bibliography: *Swarzenski, I, p. 14 f.*

54

TRÈVES, STADTBIBLIOTHEK. Cod. 31 (17,5 x 20 cm)

Apocalypse from St. Eucharius in Trèves where the manuscript was already preserved towards the end of the tenth century. Allied to the Ada group, Trèves? 8th to 9th century.

A. THE ANGEL IS SPEAKING TO ST. JOHN. (Revelations I, 1). Below is the Trèves anathema: CODEX SCI. EVCHARII PRIMI TREVIRORVM ARCHI-EPISCOPI SI QVIS EVM ABSTVLERIT ANATHEMA SIT, AMEN.

B. THE MESSAGE TO THE WRITING ST. JOHN. (Revelations X, 5). *The illustrations are drawn in brown ink and lightly washed over with minium, Naples yellow, pale blue, and red ochre. The sky is blue, often with white and red fleecy clouds and white dotted rosettes. The frame bars are in minium.*

BIBLIOGRAPHY

BOINET, pl. 153a, 154a, 155.

BRAUN, p. 49 ff.

GOLDSCHMIDT, I, p. 9.

H. OMONT, *Manuscrits illustrés de l'apocalypse aux IX et X siècles,* in *Bulletin de la Société Française de Reproductions de Manuscrits à Peintures,* p. 86 ff., ibid. further bibliography.

TH. FRIMMEL, *Die Apokalypse in den Bilderhss. d. Mittelalters,* Vienna, p. 16 ff.

55

A. VIENNA, NATIONALBIBLIOTHEK. Cod. 652 (theol. 39)
(30,7 x 40,3 cm)

HRABANUS MAURUS, DE LAUDIBUS SANCTAE CRUCIS

From St. Stephen's Monastery at Würzburg. Fulda, between 831 and 840.

FOL. 2ᵛ: DEDICATION PAGE, HRABANUS MAURUS PRESENTS HIS BOOK TO POPE GREGORY IV

Inscription on frame:

PONTIFICEM SVMMVM SALVATOR CHRISTE TVERE
ET SALVVM NOBIS PASTOREM IN SAECVLA SERVA
PRESVL VT EXIMIVS SIT RITE GREGORIVS ALME
ECCLESIAE CVSTOS DOCTORQVE FIDELIS IN AVLA.

The background from bottom to top is in ochre, pale blue and dark blue. The draperies are white (dalmatics of deacons), pale blue (under garments), green (chasuble of Pope), brown (cowl of Hrabanus) and red (cushion). The frame is red with yellow legend (cf. Hermann).

BIBLIOGRAPHY

CLEMEN, *Fulda*, p. 127.
HERMANN, p. 88 ff., ibidem further bibliography.
SCHLOSSER, p.1 ff.
ZIMMERMANN, *Fulda*, p. 85.

photo Prof. Haseloff, Kiel

B. ROM, VATICANA. REG. LAT. 124 (28 x 37 cm)

HRABANUS MAURUS, DE LAUDIBUS SANCTAE CRUCIS

Fulda, second quarter of ninth century. Chrysography on purple.

FOL. 30: SEE A.

BIBLIOGRAPHY

CLEMEN, *Fulda*, p. 126.
HASELOFF, *Egb. Psalter*, p. 128 f.
HERMANN, p. 89 ff.
SCHLOSSER, p. 1 ff.
ZIMMERMANN, *Fulda*, p. 83 ff.

56

ROME, VATICANA. Reg. lat. 124

See plate 55b

Fol. 4^v: Full length portrait of Louis le Débonnaire

Bibliography: *See plate* 55b.

57

WÜRZBURG, UNIVERSITÄTSBIBLIOTHEK

Mp. theol. fol. 66.

Gospels

were already at Würzburg towards the end of tenth century. Fulda, c. 870

Fol. 105ᵛ: The Evangelist Luke (20 x 28, 2 cm)

The undergarment is whitish, the drapery dark green, the cloak lilac.

BIBLIOGRAPHY

Beissel, *Evang. Bch.*, p. 182.
Haseloff, *Egb. Psalter*, p. 128.
Swarzenski, I, p. 6, 16 note 2, note 9, 18 sub III.
Swarzenski. II, p. 6 note 1, 32 note 1.
Zimmermann, *Fulda*, p. 72 ff., plates 10, 11.

photo Staatl. Bildstelle, Berlin

58

ERLANGEN, UNIVERSITÄTSBIBLIOTHEK. COD. 141

GOSPELS FROM ST. GUMBERT IN ANSBACH

Fulda, c. 870

FOL. 101^v: THE EVANGELIST JOHN (24, 2 x 33, 8 cm)

BIBLIOGRAPHY

BEISSEL, *Evang. Bch.*, p. 182.
BOINET, pl. 24.
HASELOFF, *Egb. Psalter*, p. 128.
SWARZENSKI, I, p. 6, 16 note 10, 18 sub III.
SWARZENSKI, II, p. 32 note 1.
ZIMMERMANN, *Fulda*, p. 66 ff., plate 8⁄9.

photo Staatl. Bildstelle, Berlin

59

MUNICH, UNIVERSITÄTSBIBLIOTHEK. Cod. fol. 29
(22,5 x 32,6 cm)

GOSPELS IN UNCIAL WRITING (PARTIALLY CHRYSOGRAPHY), FROM INGOLSTADT

The text shows the closest agreement with the later manuscripts of the Ada group. Fulda, ninth century.

FOL. 15: BEGINNING OF THE GOSPEL OF ST. MARK

In the letter I gold, blue, red and yellow tints predominant. The bust with white halo and undergarment and blue or red cloak on black ground. The background of the letter N below is red ochre with tendrils in green, yellow and white tints, above green with yellow ornamentation. The dotted lines and the triangles are in a red tint (cf. Dobschütz).

BIBLIOGRAPHY

DOBSCHÜTZ, *Studien z. Text-Kritik der Vulgata*. Leipzig, 1894, with 2 plates.
SWARZENSKI I, p. 7, 17 note 14.
ZIMMERMANN, *Fulda*, p. 82, ibid. further bibliographical references.

N

TIVM;
EVANGELII
IHV XPI FILIIDI
SICVT SCRIP
TVM EST IN
ESAIA PROPHE
TA ECCE MIT
TO ANGELVM
MEVM ANTEFA
CIEM TVAM QVI
PRAEPARAVIT VI
AM TVAM;
VOX CLAMANTIS
IN DESERTO
PARATE VIAM
DNI RECTAS
FACITE SE
MITAS EIUS

MR III
VI
MT VIII

FUIT IOHANNES IN DE
SERTO BAPTIZANS
ET PRAEDICANS BAP
TISMUM PAENITEN
TIAE IN REMIS SIO
NEM PECCATORUM
ET EGREDIEBATUR AD
ILLUM OMNIS IUDAEAE
REGIO ET HIEROSO
LYMITAE UNIUERSI
ET BAPTIZABANTUR
AB ILLO IN IORDANE
FLUMINE CONFI
TENTES PECCATA
SUA

MR IIII
XI
MT X
IO XII

ET ERAT IOHANNES
UESTITUS PILIS
CAMELI ET ZONA
PELLICIA CIRCA
LUMBOS EIUS
ET LOCUSTAS ET MEL
SILUESTRE EDE
BAT ET PRAEDICA
BAT DICENS
UENIT FORTIOR ME
POST ME CUIUS
NON SUM DIGNUS
PROCUMBENS SOL
UERE CORRIGIAM
CALCIAMENTORUM
EIUS

60

BERLIN, STAATSBIBLIOTHEK. Cod. theol. lat. fol. 1

Gospels from Herford

(so-called Cod. Wittechindeus)

Alleged to have been in sepulchral church of Wittekind at Enger. Fulda, towards 975.

A. Fol. 14ᵛ: The Evangelist Matthew (23,5 x 30,1 cm)

Ground purple on green underpainting. Drapery light green with minium lining, cloak lilac. Also for the rest the chief colours are green and lilac (architecture, drapery of the throne, angel, foliage). In addition to this there is a heavy greyish green in the shafts of the columns and in the cushion, a salmon red in the throne, and gold and silver in the details and haloes. The flesh, in narrow connection with the Ada group has light pink tints with white lights, greenish shadows and brownish violet and red lines.

B. Fol. 102ᵛ: The Evangelist John (24 x 30,2 cm)

Ground purple, with light green above and a yellow stripe in the middle. Drapery lilac with minium lining, cloak very light yellow with darker shades. Symbol dull orange, curtains shiny minium to orange, throne in orange, light green, lilac an yellow stripes. Frame chiefly light green and lilac. Details and haloes in gold and silver. The flesh as in A.

BIBLIOGRAPHY

Beissel, *Evang. Bch.,* p. 182.
Boinet, pl. 25.
Haseloff, *Egb. Psalter,* p. 128.
Goldschmidt, II, p. 17.
Swarzenski, II, p. 28 note 2.
Zimmermann, *Fulda,* p. 58 ff., 82.

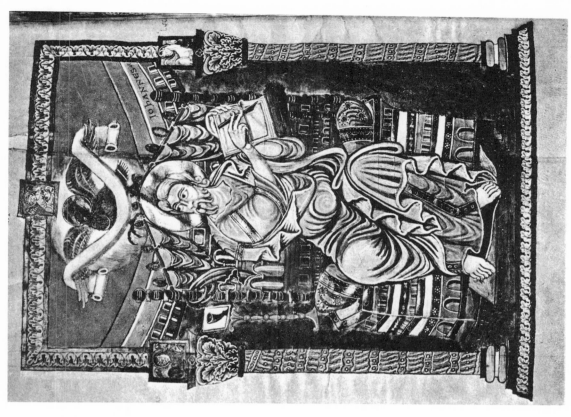

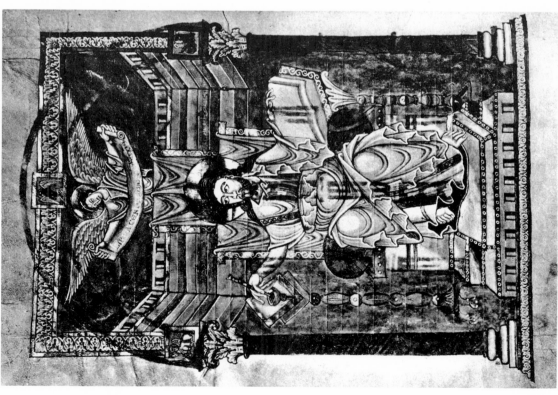

61

ROME, VATICANA. Pal. lat. 834

Miscellaneous writings: Beda, Martyrologium etc.

From the Monastery of Lorsch and perhaps there executed. Contains in the Martyrology indications pointing to Hornbach in the lower Palatinate and the Convent of St. Philip near Worms. Ninth to tenth century.

Fol. 28: Three Saints, the Trinity as indicated by contemporaneous verses on following leaf

Inscription: Haec vulgo pictura manet dignissima laude et manus eximia laude cluente simul.

Pendrawing: the third figure is distinguished by blue ink from the two others which are drawn in a dark-brown tint. In addition to the Trinity, the manuscript contains a drawing of the Crucifixion allied to that of the Vienna Otfried Ms. (see plate 62).

BIBLIOGRAPHY

Fr. Falk, *Beiträge zur Rekonstruktion d. alten Bibliotheca Fuldensis und Bibliotheca Laureshamensis - 26. Beiheft d. Zentr. Bl. f. Bibl. Wesen*, 1902, p. 66.
Hermann, I, p. 131.
Zimmermann, *Fulda*, p. 104.

Haec uulgo pictura manet dignissima laude
Et manus eximia . Laude cluente simul.

62

VIENNA, NATIONALBIBLIOTHEK. COD. 2687 (THEOL. 345)
(20,6 ⸗ 21,2 x 24,8 ⸗ 25,6 cm)

OTFRIED OF WEISSENBURG, GOSPELS

c. 868, probably executed at Weissenburg. Autograph of poet.

FOL. 153ᵛ: CRUCIFIXION WITH VIRGIN AND ST. JOHN, SUN AND MOON.
cf. text to plate 61.

The colours employed are: vigorous sorrel (the apron of Christ, cloak of St. John, halo of Virgin), minium (halo of St. John, kerchief of Virgin), dirty, thin brown (inner compartment of cross), dull olive (drapery of Virgin and Moon, cloak of Sun). Brown drawing on vellum ground. Flesh uncoloured. The hair shows various gradations of brown working up to red.

BIBLIOGRAPHY

HERMANN, I, p. 126 f., ibid. coloured plate and earlier bibliography.
ZIMMERMANN, *Fulda,* p. 103.

63

BERLIN, STAATSBIBLIOTHEK. THEOL. LAT. FOL. 58
(24 x 29,3 cm)
SO-CALLED PSALTER OF LOUIS THE GERMAN

In the frame of the two first pages: HLUDOWICO REGI VITA SALUS FE-
LICITAS PERPES.

FOL. 120: CRUCIFIXION WITH VIRGIN AND ST. JOHN, SOL AND LUNA
AND WORSHIPPER, to the Oratio ante crucem dicenda. Not belonging to
the original contents of the manuscript. South German? End of ninth century (principal part of Codex French).

*Colours: vigorous, rather bright green (Cross), slate blue (praying stool, drapery
of Sol, torch of Luna), purple brown (drapery of donor, of Virgin and Luna,
apron of Christ, cloak of St. John), yellowish minium (drapery of St. John,
horn of plenty of Sol), vigorous yellow (stockings of donor, cloaks of Sol and
Luna), brown pen drawing. Flesh vellum, shaded in red. Hair brown and black.
Vellum ground.*

BIBLIOGRAPHY

HERMANN, I, p. 131.
SCHLOSSER, p. 22.
SWARZENSKI, I, p. 14 note, 72 note.
ZIMMERMANN, *Fulda,* p. 103 f.

64

MUNICH, STAATSBIBLIOTHEK. Cod. lat. 22053 (cim. 20)
(14 x 18,5 cm)

Wessobrunn Prayer book

Part I: De inqvisitione vel inventione crucis. From Wessobrunn, whither, however, it came only at a later date. Bavarian? about 800. (prior to 814).

A. Fol. 16: Baptism of Jude

B. Fol 16ᵛ: Helena requests Jude to procure her the nails of the cross

The illustrations are drawn in brown ink and lightly coloured with minium, azure and yellow tints.

BIBLIOGRAPHY

Ada-Hs., p. 105.
A. v. Eckardt, Facsimile edition with Introduction by Karl von Kraus: *Die Handschrift des Wessobrunner Gebets,* Munich, Kurt Wolff, 1922.

photo Reusch, Munich

epo qui inillotempore erat. qui & bap
tizauit eum Inepo.

Cum mofce retur adhuc beata hit
nec inhierofolyma. factum est

Instructa aleplata fpu fco. coepit
rerum studiore Inquirere.
hic bea   bclona

65

QUEDLINBURG, STIFTSKIRCHE. Treasury-chamber
(Cover 27,9 x 37 cm)

Gospels of the presbyter Samuhel

At the end of Ms. « In nomine Domini ego Samuhel indignus vocatus presbyter scripsi istum evangelium ».

It is perhaps the same presbyter Samuhel, to whom Hrabanus Maurus addressed several poems *(Poet. lat.* II, *188).* Probably he was abbot of Lorsch, bishop of Worms in 841, *a puero ibidem (in Lorsch) educatus* and probably a schoolfellow *(sodalis)* of Hrabanus mentioned by Alcuin. He died in 855 or 856 *(cf.* Wattenbach, *Deutschlands Geschichtsquellen,* I, p. *220).* Of Samuhel's works are also preserved the Gospels at Maihingen (see plate 66) and a very similar Ms. in the library of the Bollandists at Brussels. Middle of the ninth century. The miniatures of the Evangelists are model-led on an original of the School of Tours.

The Evangelist Luke with initial page

BIBLIOGRAPHY

A. Brinkmann, *Bau- und Kunstdenkmäler des Kreises u. Stadt Quedlinburg,* 1922, p. 128 ff. ibid. reproductions.

Wilh. Köhler, *Denkmäler der karol. Kunst in Belgien - Belg. Kunstdenkmäler,* ed. by P. Clemen, I, p. 4.

Fr. Kugler, I, p. 624.

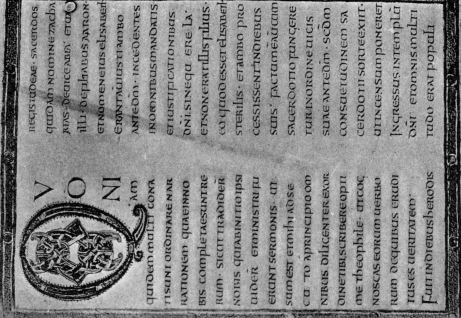

INCIPE EVANGL LUCA.

66

GOSPELS OF THE PRESBYTER SAMUHEL

SEE PLATE 65

Written by the same presbyter Samuhel as the Gospels at Quedlinburg. German. Ninth century.

FOL. 8ᵛ-9: THE EVANGELIST MATTHEW WITH INITIAL PAGE

BIBLIOGRAPHY: *See plate 65.*

67

ST. GALL, STIFTSBIBLIOTHEK. Cod. 22
Psalterium Aureum

St. Gall, latter half of the ninth century (begun prior to 883).

PAGE 14: ST. JEROME

The figure on vellum ground left uncovered, with yellow, relatively green shades and details in gold. The halo, architecture and cover of book are in emerald. The flesh-tints are unpainted, with fine minium shades. Hair is golden. Fillings of spandrels are in light yellow, emerald and olive green tints on purple ground, outlines in red. Gold and minium details.

BIBLIOGRAPHY

ADA-Hs., p. 106 f.
BOINET, pl. 144-46.
HASELOFF, *Egb. Psalter,* p. 161, 169.
LANDSBERGER, p. 25 ff., 37 ff. and passim.
MERTON, p. 38 ff., 55, 58 ff.
RUDOLF RAHN, *Das Psalterium Aureum von St. Gallen,* with coloured plates.
    St. Gall 1878.
SWARZENSKI II, p. 116 note 2, 132 notes 1 and 3.

photo Stoedtner, Berlin

68

A. ST. GALL, STIFTSBIBLIOTHEK. Cod. 22

SEE PLATE 67

PAGE 2: KING DAVID WITH HIS MUSICIANS

Colours: Figures as in plate 67. Foreground bright ochre. Plate of footstool minium. The ground within the arcade is green with gold, the upper part purple with gold (cf. the figures on plate 68B).

BIBLIOGRAPHY: *See plate 67.*

photo Stoedtner, Berlin

B. PARIS, BIBLIOTHÈQUE NATIONALE. Ms. lat. 1152

PSALTER OF CHARLES THE BALD

Executed by the scribe Liuthard for Charles the Bald. From the cathedral of Metz, where the manuscript must already have been preserved towards the end of the tenth century. So-called school of Corbie, (better St. Denis). Between 842 and 869 (probably towards the end of this period).

Fol. 1ᵛ: THE MUSICIANS OF KING DAVID

BIBLIOGRAPHY

ADA-Hs., p. 97.
BOINET, pl. 113-114.
GOLDSCHMIDT, I, p. 23 ff.

69

ST. GALL, STIFTSBIBLIOTHEK. COD. 22

SEE PLATE 67

PAGE 141: SIEGE AND CAPTURE OF A CITY (Rabbath? II. Samuel XII, 26 ff.)

Brown pen drawing lightly washed over in the shades with minium, purple, emerald, bright ochre and pale bluish grey.

BIBLIOGRAPHY: *See plate 67.*

photo Stoedtner, Berlin

70

A. ST. GALL, STIFTSBIBLIOTHEK. COD. 22

SEE PLATE 67

PAGE 17: B(EATUS VIR)

The ground is purple, in the plaitwork knots and corners of frame, a green tint is used and the ornaments are in gold. The borders with staircase pattern are in bright yellow and green. Minium drawing.

BIBLIOGRAPHY: *See plate 67.*

photo Staatl. Bildstelle, Berlin (Merton)

B. ST. GALL, STIFTSBIBLIOTHEK. COD. 23

FOLCHARD-PSALTER (SEE PLATE 71)

PAGE 315: INITIAL D(OMINE)

Gold and silver on blue and green ground. Minium drawing.

BIBLIOGRAPHY: *See plate 71.*

photo Staatl. Bildstelle, Berlin (Merton)

71

ST. GALL, STIFTSBIBLIOTHEK. COD. 23 (29 x 38,5 cm)
PSALTER OF FOLCHARD

So called after the Scribe, cf. the legend on p. 26 and 27:

> HUNC PRAECEPTORIS HARTMOTI JUSSA SECUTUS
> FOLCHARDUS STUDUIT RITE PATRARE LIBRUM.

St. Gall, third quarter of the ninth century (before 872).

A. TWO SAINTS IN HALF FIGURE (Cut from a litany-page)

Writing: Gold and silver on purple, lunette ground blue or green, arcades and fillings in spandrels principally gold and silver with minium drawing, blue and green. Figures left open in brown pen drawing, lightly touched up with green, red and violet.

B. THE RETURN OF THE ARK OF THE COVENANT (II. Sam. VI, 1-5)

Colours as in A., but body colour laid on more thickly in figures. The figures in lunettes are red, green and purple, those of the spandrels gold, and silver on purple (cf. Landsberger).

BIBLIOGRAPHY

ADA-HS., p. 106.
BOINET, pl. 141-43.
HASELOFF, *Egb. Psalter,* p. 169.
LANDSBERGER, ibid. further bibliography.
MERTON, p. 33 ff., 41, 55, 57 ff.
STETTINER, p. 90, 93; plate 165.

photo Staatl. Bildstelle, Berlin (Merton)

OMNES III
TENICIUES·OR
OMS·S·PATRIAR
CHE·OR·P·N

OMS·S·VIDUE
OR·P·NOBIS·
OMS·S·POENITEN
TES·OR·PRO·N

ABIRATUA·LIB
AUINSIDIIS·INIMI
CI·LIB·NOS·DNE
ASUBITANEA·MOR
TE·LIB·NOS·DNE

AMORBO·MALO·E·
PCRUCE·TUA·E·
PPASSIONE·TUA·E·
PRESURREC·TUA·E·
PASCENSIONE·TUA·E·

72

LEYDEN, UNIVERSITY LIBRARY. Cod. Perizoni 17
(17,6 x 25,5 cm)
Book of Maccabees

St. Gall, first half of the tenth century (with additions from Reichenau, of middle of the tenth century).

Fol. 9: Illustration to I. Mac. 1, 30 ff.

The King sends his treasurer against Jerusalem (below); and the storming of a city (probably Jerusalem).

Brown pen drawing, small portions in red, green, yellow and blue tints or painted over with silver.

BIBLIOGRAPHY

Haseloff, *Egb. Psalter*, p. 161 note 2.
Merton, p. 64 ff.
Swarzenski II, p. 134 note 6.

photo Staatl. Bildstelle, Berlin (Merton)

73

FOL. 9: MATHATHIAS SLAYS THE CHIEFTAIN OF ANTIOCHUS and the Jew who is sacrificing to the idols (I. Mac. II, 23-25; cf. I, 50).

COLOURS AND BIBLIOGRAPHY: *See plate 72.*

photo Staatl. Bildstelle, Berlin (Merton)

74

BERN, STADTBIBLIOTHEK. Cod. 264 (21 x 27,5 cm)
PRUDENTIUS, PSYCHOMACHIA

St. Gall? tenth century.

FOL. 33: ABRAHAM AND THE THREE ANGELS
Brown pen drawing, touched over with colour (principally with purple).

BIBLIOGRAPHY

MERTON, p. 61 f., 68, 83.
STETTINER, p. 70 ff., plate 129-164.

photo Staatl. Bildstelle, Berlin (Merton)

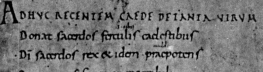

ADHVC RECENTEM CAEDE DETANIA VIRVM

Donat sacerdos ferculis cadestibus

Di sacerdos rex & idem praepotens

Origo cuius fonte inenarrabili

Scorta nullum pdit auctorem fui

Melchisedech qua stirpe quis maiorib.

Ignotus ani cognitus tantum do

OX TITRIFORMIS ANGELOR TRINITAS

Senis reuisit hospitiis mappalia

Etiam quietam sarrae maluum sterile

Munus uouit mater exsanguis stupet

75

BERN, STADTBIBLIOTHEK. COD. 264
SEE PLATE 74

FOL. 42: SUPERBIA.

Above: restlessly bounding to and fro *(Psychomachia V, v. 120⁄193)*;
below: threatening Humilitas and Spes *(Psychomachia V, v. 194⁄252)*.

COLOURS AND BIBLIOGRAPHY: *See plate* 74.

photo Staatl. Bildstelle, Berlin (Merton)

Aceruice fluens tenui uelamine limbuf

Concipit ingestas textis tangentibus auras

N ecmin instabilis sonipes feritate superbit

Impatiens madidis frenaries ora lupatis

Huc illuc frendens obuertit tergu negata

Libertate fuge pressisq uonescit habenis

& Hocese ostentuis habitu neruosa uirago

Int utraq acie sup eminet & falerorum

Cirtusflectit equu uultu q & uoce minac

76

ROME, VATICANA. Reg. lat. 438 (14,5 x 29 cm)

CALENDAR OF THE WANDALBERT MARTYROLOGY

According to Riegl perhaps from Monastery of Prüm (rather Alamannic, St. Gall?). Beginning of the tenth century.

A. MONTH OF MAY

Inscription: «Majus agenorei miratur cornua tauri».

B. MONTH OF NOVEMBER

Inscription: «Scorpius hibernam praeceps iubet ire novembrem».

The miniatures are drawn with the pen, and painted over in green and red, little yellow and blue, and also much gold. Above the colour, the pen strokes in many places have been traced afterwards in red and gold.

BIBLIOGRAPHY

ALOIS RIEGL, *Die mittelalterl. Kalender-Illustr. - Mitt. d. Inst f. österr. Gesch.- Forschung*, X, 1889, No 1, p. 400, ff. with plates.

BRAUN, p. 87.

HASELOFF, *Malerschule*, p. 73 f.

SWARZENSKI II, p. 18 note 2.

photo Prof. Haseloff, Kiel

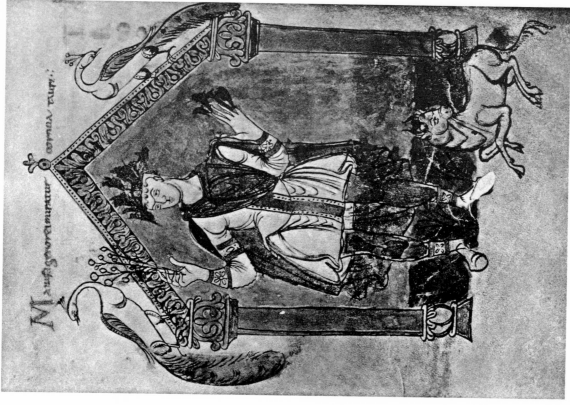

77

ZÜRICH, STADTBIBLIOTHEK. Ms. C. XII (23 x 31 cm)
PSALTER

St. Gall, first half of the ninth century.

FOL. 53: PENANCE OF DAVID BEFORE NATHAN (Before Ps. LI).

The Codex contains initials of a Merovingian character; in the colours there are Naples yellow, minium and sap green.

BIBLIOGRAPHY: *Merton*, p. 15 ff., 41, 55.

photo Staatl. Bildstelle, Berlin (Merton)

ontritum & humili ceru dñr derpi
nigne fee dñe m bonce uo   ecier:
um tecre tuccsion: &cedi ficen
tur muri hierureclem   ;.
ne ccceptcebir scceri ficium iursti
icce oblccctioner & holocccusteu
tunc mponeri super cltcore tu
um uitulos :-

78

ST. GALL, STIFTSBIBLIOTHEK. COD. 64 (17,2 x 21 cm)

EPISTLES OF ST. PAUL

St. Gall, first half of the tenth century.

PAGE 12: DERISION OF ST. PAUL. *Brown pen drawing.*

BIBLIOGRAPHY

STETTINER, p. 90 ff., pl. 166.
LANDSBERGER, p. 37 note 4.
MERTON, p. 60 f., 84.

photo Staatl. Bildstelle, Berlin (Merton)

ARGVMENTVM EPLE ADROMANOS · PRESENS TEXTVS ·
HABET MERITIS VT GRA DIFFERT REDDENS CONCORDES
REBECCE VENTRE FREQVENTES.

PAVLVS

IVDEI ET
GENTES

79

STUTTGART, LANDESBIBLIOTHEK. Cod. II, 54
(20,5 x 30 cm)
Epistles of St. Paul, Acts, Apocalypse

The manuscript came to Stuttgart from the Cathedral Library of Constance by way of Weingarten. St. Gall, beginning of the ninth century.

Fol. 24: St. Paul writing (The letters in the book are a later addition).

Drawn in dark brown ink, all contours edged with a line in red; tunic and border of book are lightly washed with yellow.

BIBLIOGRAPHY

Merton, p. 18 f., 55, 57, 88.

photo Staatl. Bildstelle, Berlin (Merton)

SCS PAVLUS

Sedet hic Scripsit

80

ST. GALL, STIFTSBIBLIOTHEK. COD. 90 (25,5 x 32 cm)

COLLECTION OF MISCELLANEOUS WRITINGS

including the Astronomy of Aratus. (In the same library is also found a
St. Gall copy of the Codex executed in the tenth century: Cod. 250;
cf. plate 14). St. Gall, middle of the ninth century.

PAGE 76: CELESTIAL CHART. *Brown pen-drawing.*

BIBLIOGRAPHY

MERTON, p. 56 f. note 49.
GEORG THIELE, *Antike Himmelsbilder,* 1898, p. 160 f.

photo Staatl. Bildstelle, Berlin (Merton)

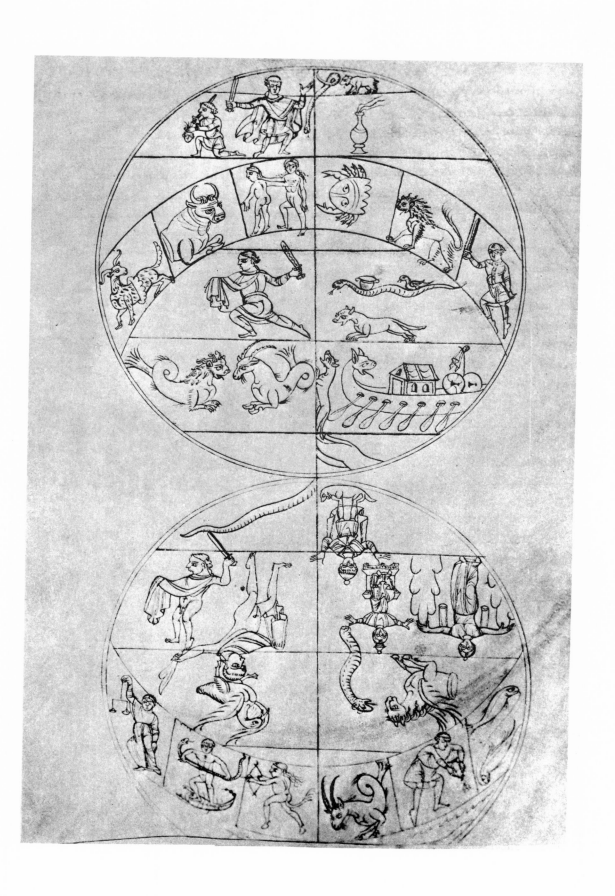

81

CASSEL, LANDESBIBLIOTHEK. Cod. theol. fol. 60
(19,5 x 24,5 cm)
Gospels

From the Monastery of Abdinghof near Paderborn. Region of the Weser?
tenth century.

Fol. 12: Maiestas Domini. *Brown pen-drawing.*

BIBLIOGRAPHY

Beissel, *Evang. Bch.*, p. 290.
Kugler, I, p. 52.
Ludorff, *Kunstdenkmäler von Westfalen, Kreis Paderborn,* p. 107 f. with repr.
Swarzenski II, p. 113 note 1.
Zimmermann, *Fulda,* p. 101.

82

CASSEL, LANDESBIBLIOTHEK. Cod. theol. fol. 60

See plate 81

A. Fol. 1: Crucifixion with St. Mary and St. John, Terra, Sol and Luna

B. Fol. 2: The women at the Tomb and the Harrowing of Hell

Colours and Bibliography: *See plate* 81.

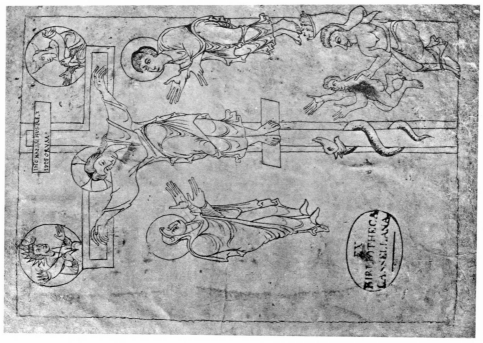

83

A. BERLIN, STAATSBIBLIOTHEK. Cod. theol. lat. quart. 5
(21,5 x 26 cm)

GOSPELS FROM ST. MAURITIUS IN MAGDEBURG

Saxon? tenth to eleventh century.

FOL. 9: THE EVANGELIST MATTHEW. *Brown pen-drawing.*

BIBLIOGRAPHY

VAL. ROSE, *Verzeichniss d. lat. Hss. d. Kgl. Bibl. zu Berlin, II, No. 267.*

B. MUNICH, STAATSBIBLIOTHEK. Cod. lat. 10077. (CIM. 143)
(17,5 x 25,5 cm)

SACRAMENTARY FROM THE CATHEDRAL TREASURY OF VERDUN

Written for the abbey of Corvey. Fulda or Corvey? tenth to eleventh century.

FOL. 105ᵛ: FRAGMENTARY REPRESENTATION OF PENTECOST
(for the office of Pentecost). Corresponds to the upper part of the representation of the Feast of Pentecost in the Gospels from Abdinghof preserved at Cassel (cf. Vol. II, plate 111, which shows a crucifixion of the same manuscript). *Brown pen-drawing.*

BIBLIOGRAPHY

PAUL LEHMANN, *Corveyer Stud.-Abhdlg. d. Bayr. Akad. d. Wiss. Phil.-Hist. Kl.* Nr. xxx, Abh. 5, p. 40 ff.
SWARZENSKI, I, p. 17 note 13, 93 note.
ZIMMERMANN, *Fulda,* p. 35 ff.

photo Reusch, Munich

IN PENTECOSTEN

DOMINICA SCA

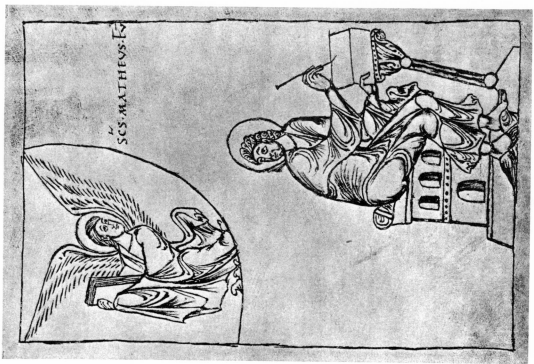

SCS·MATHEVS·E

84

LEIPZIG, STADTBIBLIOTHEK. Cod. CXC

Two separate leaves of a Sacramentary stitched in into an Evangelistary of Reichenau of the tenth century. Alamannic? tenth century.

A. FOL. 1ᵛ: CRUCIFIX BETWEEN VIRGIN AND ST. JOHN (15,8 x 27 cm)

Inscription of frame:

> FVLGIDA STELLA MARIS
> PRO CVNCTIS POSCE MISELLIS
> ET TV IVNGE PRECES
> CVM VIRGINE VIRGO JOHANNES
> ANNVAT HOC AGNVS
> MVNDI PRO PESTE PEREMPTVS

Inscription of the background:

> IN CRVCE XPE TVA
> CONFIGE NOCENTIA CVNCTA
> STELLA MARIS
> VIRGO JOHANNIS

The figures drawn in brown and uncoloured on a dark purple ground. The letters are white, cross and halo are green, the plate for the inscription and the frame are blue.

B. FOL. 2: ST. GREGORY (15 x 20 cm). On the book: « SCRIBIT GREGORIUS DICTAT QUAE SP(IRITU)S ALMUS ».

Colours as in A. *The pattern of the ground is white, the frame green.*

BIBLIOGRAPHY

ROBERT BRUCK, *Malereien in Hss. d. Kgr. Sachsen*, p. 12, Dresden, 1906.
MERTON, p. 83, 88., ibid. further bibliography.
ZIMMERMANN, *Fulda*, p. 101.

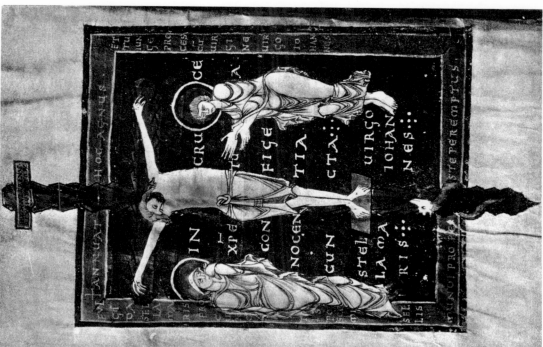

85

WOLFENBÜTTEL, LANDESBIBLIOTHEK
16. 1. AUG. FOL. HEINEMANN 2187 (22 x 32,5 cm)
GOSPELS

Contains a number of indications referring to Speyer and was bought at Worms in 1596. Region of the Weser? tenth century.

FOL. 9: ANNUNCIATION TO THE SHEPHERDS. *Brown pen-drawing.*

BIBLIOGRAPHY

O. VON HEINEMMANN, *Die Hss. d. Hzgl. Bibl. zu Wolfenbüttel,* II, 2, p. 204.
ZIMMERMANN, *Fulda,* p. 101.

86

WOLFENBÜTTEL, LANDESBIBLIOTHEK
16. I. AUG. FOL. HEINEMANN 2187

SEE PLATE 85

FOL. 18: ADORATION OF THE MAGI

COLOURS AND BIBLIOGRAPHY:

See plate 85.

87

ZÜRICH, STADTBIBLIOTHEK. Ms. C. 80 (17,8 x 24 cm)

DIALECTIC AND RHETORIC OF ALBINUS

(from St. Gall) St. Gall or region of the Weser (?). The Codex is of the
ninth century, the drawing of the middle of the tenth century.

FOL. 83: MAIESTAS DOMINI. *Brown pen-drawing.*

BIBLIOGRAPHY

MERTON, p. 63 f.

photo Staatl. Bildstelle, Berlin (Merton)

88

DÜSSELDORF, LANDESBIBLIOTHEK. A. 44

PAULI EPISTOLAE

According to Köhler it is probably Rhenish (Coblenz?) about 850. In the text also a continental Anglo-Saxon script was used.

FOL. 120: ST. PAUL

Inscription: PAVLVS IAM DVDVM SAVLVS PROCERVM PRECEPTA SECVTVS

Brown pen-drawing. Such a daring position is doubtless not an invention of the draughtsman but a copy of a late antique model (perhaps by way of England.) The inventor evidently had the idea that St. Paul sitting in front has turned towards the hand of God stretching out to him from the distance. The plate of the writing desk is lying across his knees, while the scroll is spread over it.

BIBLIOGRAPHY

P. CLEMEN, *Kunstdenkmäler der Rheinprovinz,* III, 1, p. 69, N. 5.

photo Deutscher Verein f. Kunstw.

IAM DUDUM SAULUS PROCERÃ
PRECEP TA SECUTUS

paulus

GERMAN ILLUMINATION

GERMAN ILLUMINATION

BY

ADOLPH GOLDSCHMIDT

Professor in the University of Berlin

VOLUME II

OTTONIAN PERIOD

CONTENTS

LIST OF PLATES

14 A. COBLENZ, STAATSARCHIV. Cod. 701. Gospels from Sta. Maria ad Martyres at Trèves. *Maiestas Domini.*
B. BERLIN, STAATSBIBLIOTHEK. Cod. theol. lat. fol. 283. See plate 13B. *Christ enthroned on the Globe.*

15 PARIS, BIBLIOTHÈQUE NATIONALE. Cod. 10501. Sacramentary. The Saints point to Trèves. A. *Beginning of the canon-table.* T(E IGITUR). B. *Crucifixion and continuation of the canon-table.*

16 A. PARIS, BIBLIOTHÈQUE NATIONALE. Cod. lat. 8851. See plate 9. *Title page to St. Matthew with four Ottonian busts, probably of Henry I, Otto I and II.*
B. MANCHESTER, RYLANDS LIBRARY 98. Gospels. *Ornamented page (beginning of St. Matthew) with miniatures of the Ottonian Emperors on the margin.*

17 DARMSTADT, LANDESBIBLIOTHEK. Cod. 1948. Sacramentary of Gero. A. *Gero presents the manuscript to St. Peter.* B. *Maiestas Domini.*

18 A. KARLSBURG (GYULAFEHÉRVÁR), ROUMANIA, BATTHYÁNEUM. Gospels of St. Matthew and St. Mark. *The Evangelist Matthew.*
B. DARMSTADT, LANDESBIBLIOTHEK. Cod. 1948. See plate 17. *The Evangelist Matthew.*

19 HEIDELBERG, UNIVERSITY LIBRARY. Cod. Sal. ixb. Sacramentary from Petershausen. A. *The enthroned Virgin or Ecclesia.* B. *Maiestas Domini.*

20 CIVIDALE, BIBLIOTECA. Cod. Gertrudianus. Psalter. *King David.*

21 CIVIDALE, BIBLIOTECA. Cod. Gertrudianus. See plate 20. A. *St. Valerius.* B. *Initial B(EATI) to Ps. XXXI.*

22 PARIS, BIBLIOTHÈQUE NATIONALE. Ms. Lat. 10514. Gospels from the abbey of Poussay. A. *The abbot between two angels.* B. *The Ascension of Christ.*

23 SOLOTHURN, SACRISTY OF THE COLLEGIATSTIFT. Sacramentary. *Presentation of the book to Christ by St. Peter.*

24 MUNICH, STAATSBIBLIOTHEK. Cod. lat. 4453. (Cim. 58). Gospels from the Cathedral treasury at Bamberg. A. *The provinces paying homage to the Emperor (Slavinia, Germania, Gallia and Roma).* B. *The enthroned Emperor (probably Otto III) and his suite.*

25 MUNICH, STAATSBIBLIOTHEK. Cod. lat. 4453. See plate 24. *The Evangelist Matthew.*

26 MUNICH, STAATSBIBLIOTHEK. Cod. lat. 4453. See plate 24. *The Evangelist Luke.*

27 MUNICH, STAATSBIBLIOTHEK. Cod. lat. 4453. See plate 24. *The Baptism and the three temptations of Christ.*

28 MUNICH, STAATSBIBLIOTHEK. Cod. lat. 4453. See plate 24. *The parable of the Good Samaritan.*

29 MUNICH, STAATSBIBLIOTHEK. Cod. lat. 4453. See plate 24. *The Washing of the feet.*

30 BAMBERG, STAATSBIBLIOTHEK. Cod. bibl. 76 (A. I. 43). Commentary on Isaiah from the Cathedral at Bamberg. *Vision of Isaiah.*

31 BAMBERG, STAATSBIBLIOTHEK. Cod. bibl. 22 (A. I. 47). Commentary on Daniel from the Bamberg Cathedral library. *Initial A(NNO) with the writing Daniel.*

32 ROME, VATICANA. Barb. lat. 711 (formerly XIV, 84). Evangelistary. *The Evangelist John.*

33 ROME, VATICANA. Barb. lat. 711. See plate 32. *The Nativity of Christ with the shepherds adoring and the Annunciation to the shepherds.*

34 MUNICH, STAATSBIBLIOTHEK. Cod. lat. 23338. Evangelistary. *Parable of the debtor (according to Matth. XVIII, 23-35).*

35 MUNICH, STAATSBIBLIOTHEK. Cod. lat. 4452 (Cim. 57). Gospels from the Cathedral treasury at Bamberg. A. *The Evangelist Matthew.* B. *The Evangelist Mark.*

36 MUNICH, STAATSBIBLIOTHEK. Cod. lat. 4452. See plate 35. *Annunciation to the Shepherds.*

37 MUNICH, STAATSBIBLIOTHEK. Cod. lat. 4452. See plate 35. *Last Supper and Washing of the feet.*

38 A. MUNICH, STAATSBIBLIOTHEK. Cod. lat. 4452. See plate 35. *Initials IN (PRINCIPIO ERAT).*
B. MUNICH, STAATSBIBLIOTHEK. Cod. lat. 4454 (Cim. 59). Gospels from Bamberg. *Initials IN (PRINCIPIO ERAT).*

39 BAMBERG, STAATSBIBLIOTHEK. Cod. bibl. 140 (A. II. 42). Apocalypse and Evangelistary from St. Stephen's in Bamberg. *The beast and the false prophet thrown into hell, the others are slain with the sword (Revelations XIX, 20 and 21).*

40 MUNICH, Staatsbibliothek. Cod. lat. 4454 (Cim. 59). Gospels from the Cathedral treasury of Bamberg (cf. plate 38 B). A. *The Evangelist Mark with the rising Christ.* B. *The Evangelist John with the Ascension of Christ.*

41 COLOGNE, Cathedral Library, 218. Gospels from the monastery Limburg on the Hardt. *The Apostle John.*

42 COLOGNE, Cathedral Library, 218. See plate 41. Q(uoniam quidem).

43 GOTHA, Landesbibliothek. I, 19. Cod. aureus. Gospels of Otto III. *Maiestas Domini with the symbols of the Evangelists and the four major prophets (cf. plate 9).*

44 GOTHA, Landesbibliothek. I, 19. See plate 43. A. *St. Matthew.* B. *St. Mark as bishop.*

45 GOTHA, Landesbibliothek. I, 19. See plate 43. *The Evangelist John.*

46 GOTHA, Landesbibliothek. I, 19. See plate 43. *Annunciation, Visitation, Nativity. Adoration of the Shepherds. The visit of the Kings to Herod.*

47 GOTHA, Landesbibliothek. I, 19. See plate 43. *Canon-Table.*

48 GOTHA, Landesbibliothek. I, 19. See plate 43. *Ornamented page with textile patterns.*

49 A. GOTHA, Landesbibliothek, I, 19. See plate 43. *Initial page* B(eato papae Damaso).
B. MADRID, Escorial. Cod. Aureus. Gospels from Speyer. *Initial page* B(eatissimo papae Damaso).

50 PARIS, Bibliothèque Nationale. Nouv. acquis. 2196. Gospels from Luxeuil (fragment). *The Evangelist Mark.*

51 PARIS, Bibliothèque Nationale. Cod. lat. 10438. Gospels. A. *Annunciation.* B. *Birth of Christ.*

52 BREMEN, Stadtbibliothek. Book of Pericopes of Henry III. A. *A monk and a layman.* B. *Dedication of the manuscript.*

53 BREMEN, Stadtbibliothek. See plate 52. A. *Representation of the Empress Gisela.* B. *Representation of Henry.*

54 BREMEN, Stadtbibliothek. See plate 52. A. *The healing of the blind at Jericho.* (Luke XVIII, 31-43). B. *The doubting Thomas* (John XX, 26-29).

55 BREMEN, STADTBIBLIOTHEK. See plate 52. *The parable of the Supper (Luke XVI, 16-24).*

56 BRUSSELS, BIBLIOTHÈQUE ROYALE. Cod. 9428. Lectionary. A. *Healing of the Leper.* B. *The Finding of the four Coffins with Relics of the Saints Stephanus, Nicodemus, Gamaliel and his son Abibas.*

57 MADRID, ESCORIAL. Cod. Aureus. Gospels from Speyer. *Enthroned Christ with the Imperial pair Conrad and Gisela.*

58 MADRID, ESCORIAL. Cod. Aureus. See plate 57. *The enthroned Virgin with Henry III and Agnes.*

59 MADRID, ESCORIAL. Cod. Aureus. See plate 57. *The Evangelist John.*

60 MADRID, ESCORIAL. Cod. Aureus. See plate 57. *Jesus helps His disciples in the storm (Matth. XVI, 24; Mark VI, 48).*

61 MADRID, ESCORIAL. Cod. Aureus. See plate 57. *Raising of the youth at Nain.*

62 MADRID, ESCORIAL. Cod. Aureus. See plate 57. *Parable of the Good Samaritan.*

63 UPSALA, UNIVERSITY LIBRARY. Gospels of Henry III. *Christ crowns Henry and Agnes.*

64 UPSALA, UNIVERSITY LIBRARY. Gospels of Henry III. See plate 63. *Henry presents the manuscript to Simon and Jude, the patron saints of the Cathedral of Goslar.*

65 UPSALA, UNIVERSITY LIBRARY. Gospels of Henry III. See plate 63. *The Evangelist Luke.*

66 UPSALA, UNIVERSITY LIBRARY. See plate 63. *The Evangelist John.*

67 PARIS, BIBLIOTHÈQUE NATIONALE. Cod. lat. 9448. Antiphonary from Prüm. A. *Presentation in the Temple.* B. *Dormition of the Virgin.*

68 PARIS, BIBLIOTHÈQUE NATIONALE. Cod. lat. 9448. See plate 67. A. *The two Apostles and Simon Magus before Nero.* B. *The Martyrdom of St. Peter and Paul.*

69 MANCHESTER, RYLANDS LIBRARY. No 7. Lectionary from Prüm. *The symbol of St. Matthew.*

70 MANCHESTER, RYLANDS LIBRARY. No 7. See plate 69. *Entry into Jerusalem.*

71 MANCHESTER, RYLANDS LIBRARY. No 7. See plate 69. *The Maries at the Tomb.*

72 MUNICH, Staatsbibliothek. Cod. lat. 4456. Sacramentary of Henry II. *The coronation of Henry by Christ.*

73 MUNICH, Staatsbibliothek. Cod. lat. 4456. See plate 72. *Henry II with the provinces paying homage.*

74 MUNICH, Staatsbibliothek. Cod. lat. 4456. See plate 72. *St. Gregory.*

75 MUNICH, Staatsbibliothek. Cod. lat. 4456. See plate 72. *Crucifix with the Virgin and St. John, Sol and Luna.*

76 MUNICH, Staatsbibliothek. Cod. lat. 13601. Evangelistary of Uota. *The Abbess Uota hands over the Ms. to the Virgin.*

77 MUNICH, Staatsbibliothek. Cod. lat. 13601. See plate 76. A. *Crucifix with Vita and Mors, Ecclesia and Synagoga.* B. *St. Erhard with a celebrant at the Sacrifice of the Mass.*

78 ROME, Vaticana. Ottob. lat. 74. Gospels of Henry II. *Emperor Henry II and above him the Dove of the Holy Ghost.*

79 BAMBERG, Staatsbibliothek. Cod. Bibl. 95 (A. II. 46). Gospels from Seeon. A. *King Henry II.* B. *Virgin.*

80 COLOGNE, Cathedral Library. Cod. 143. Epistolary. *The Archbishop Everger in adoration before the Apostles SS. Peter and Paul.*

81 PARIS, Bibliothèque Nationale. Cod. lat. 817. Sacramentary. A. *Maiestas Domini.* B. *Crucifix between the Virgin and St. John.*

82 COLOGNE, Stadtarchiv. Cod. 312. Gospels from St. Gereon in Cologne. A. *The Evangelist Matthew.* B. *The Evangelist John.*

83 MILAN, Ambrosiana. Cod. 53 sup. Gospels. A. *The Evangelist Luke.* B. *The Evangelist Matthew.*

84 A. MILAN, Ambrosiana. Cod. 53 sup. See plate 83. *St. Jerome offers a scroll to a deacon.*
B. GIESSEN, University Library. Cod. 660. Gospels. *St. Jerome with his scribe.*

85 GIESSEN, University Library. Cod. 660. See plate 84 B. *Crucifixion (at the beginning of the Gospels of St. John).*

86 DARMSTADT, Landesbibliothek. Cod. 1640. Gospels of the Abbess Hitda of Meschede (Westphalia). A. *The Evangelist John.* B. *The Evangelist Mark.*

87 DARMSTADT, Landesbibliothek. Cod. 1640. See plate 86. A. *Storm on the sea.* B. *The Baptism of Christ.*

88 STUTTGART, Landesbibliothek. Cod. bibl. 402. Gospels of Gundold. *The Crucifixion with the Virgin, St. John and the founder.*

89 STUTTGART, Landesbibliothek. Cod. bibl. 402. See plate 88. *Maiestas Domini with the symbols of the Evangelists and the four major prophets.*

90 A. STUTTGART, Landesbibliothek. Cod. bibl. 402. See plate 88. *The Evangelist John.*
B. DARMSTADT, Landesmuseum. A. E. 679. Gospels from St. Andreas at Cologne. *The Evangelist Mark.*

91 COLOGNE, Priesterseminar. Cod. 753b. Gospels from Sta. Maria ad Gradus in Cologne. *Maiestas Domini, with the symbols of the Evangelists and the four major prophets.*

92 BAMBERG, Staatsbibliothek. Cod. bibl. 94 (A. II. 18). Gospels. A. *Maiestas Domini with the symbols of the Evangelists and the four major prophets.* B. *Christ as world-redeemer.*

93 BAMBERG, Staatsbibliothek. Cod. bibl. 94 (A. II. 18). See plate 92. A. *The Evangelist Matthew.* B. *The Evangelist John.*

94 STUTTGART, Landesbibliothek. Cod. bibl. fol. 21. Gospels from St. Gereon in Cologne. A. *The Evangelist Mark.* B. *The Evangelist Matthew.*

95 BERLIN, Kupferstichkabinett der Staatl. Museen. Ms. 78 A 3. Gospels from the abbey of Abdinghof near Paderborn. *Mission of Christ to the Apostles (Mark XVI, 15).*

96 A. BERLIN, Kupferstichkabinett der Staatl. Museen. Ms. 79 A 3. See plate 95. *Maiestas Domini.*
B. FREIBURG (Baden), University Library. Ms. 360a. Sacramentary. *Crucifix.*

97 MUNICH, Staatsbibliothek. Cod. lat. 9475 (Cim. 142). Gospels. A. *The Evangelist Matthew.* B. *The Evangelist John.*

98 MANCHESTER, Rylands Library. Cod. No 87 (Haigh Hall 17). Gospels. A. *The Evangelist Mark.* B. *The Symbol of St. John.*

99 HILDESHEIM, Cathedral treasury. No 18. Gospels written at the request of Bishop Bernward of Hildesheim. *The Evangelist Mark.*

BIBLIOGRAPHY WITH ABBREVIATIONS

BANGE, *Abdinghof* ⁄ E. F. BANGE, *Das Abdinghofer Evangeliar im Kupferstichkabinett* — Berichte aus den Preuss. Kunstsammlg., XLII (1921), Heft 9/10.

BANGE, *frühroman. Hs.* ⁄ E. F. BANGE, *Eine frühromanische Evangelien-Handschrift mit Malereien des Hildesheimer Kunstkreises* — Monatshefte für Kunstwissensch. 1922. I, p.1.

BANGE, *Malerschule* ⁄ E. F. BANGE, *Eine bayerische Malerschule des XI. u. XII. Jhrb.*, München, Hugo Schmidt, 1923.

BEISSEL, *Bernward Evang.* ⁄ STEPHAN BEISSEL, S. J., *Des heil. Bernward Evangelienbuch.* Hildesheim, 1891.

BEISSEL, *St. Bernward* ⁄ STEPHAN BEISSEL, S. J., *Der heilige Bernward v. Hildesheim als Künstler und Förderer der deutschen Kunst.* Hildesheim, 1899.

BEISSEL, *Evang. Bch.* ⁄ STEPHAN BEISSEL, S. J., *Geschichte der Evangelienbücher in der ersten Hälfte des Mittelalters* — Stimmen aus Maria Laach, Erg. Bd. XXIII, Freiburg, 1906.

BEISSEL, *Otto-Hs.* ⁄ STEPHAN BEISSEL, S. J., *Die Bilder der Handschrift des Kaisers Otto im Münster zu Aachen.* Aachen, Barth, 1886.

BEISSEL, *Upsala* ⁄ STEPHAN BEISSEL, S. J., *Das Evangelienbuch Heinrichs III. aus dem Dome zu Goslar in der Bibliothek zu Upsala.* Düsseldorf, Schwann, 1900. (Erweiterter Abdruck aus der Zeitschrift f. christl. Kunst, XIII, with repr.).

BEISSEL, *Vat. Min.* ⁄ STEPHAN BEISSEL, S. J. *Vatikanische Miniaturen* — Quellen zur Geschichte der Buchmalerei, Freiburg, 1893.

BERNATH ⁄ M. BERNATH, *Malerei des Mittelalters* — Woltmann u. Woermann, Geschichte der Malerei I. Leipzig, 1916

BOECKLER ⁄ ALBERT BOECKLER, *Die Reichenauer Buchmalerei* — Die Kultur der Reichenau. Erinnerungsschrift zur 1200sten Wiederkehr des Gründungsjahres des Inselklosters, S. 956. München, 1925.

BRAUN ⁄ EDMUND BRAUN, *Beiträge zur Geschichte der Trierer Buchmalerei im frühen Mittelalter* — Westdeutsche Zeitschrift für Geschichte u. Kunst, Erg. Heft IX (1895).

CHROUST ⁄ ANTON CHROUST, *Monumenta Palaeographica* — Denkmäler der Schreib-kunst des Mittelalters. Ser. I, 1902-06; Ser. II, 1911-17. München.

CLEMEN, *Rom. Mon. Malerei* ⁄ PAUL CLEMEN, *Die Romanische Monumentalmalerei in den Rheinlanden,* Düsseldorf, Schwann, 1916.

DE WALD ⁄ ERNEST T. DE WALD, *The Art of the Scriptorium of Einsiedeln* — The Art Bulletin VII (1895), No. 3.

EHL ⁄ HEINRICH EHL, *Die Kölner ottonische Buchmalerei* — Forschungen zur Kunstge⁄ schichte Westeuropas, hsg. v. Eugen Lüthgen, Bd. VI. Bonn u. Leipzig, 1922.

FISCHER ⁄ HANS FISCHER, *Mittelalterliche Miniaturen aus der Staatlichen Bibliothek in Bamberg,* Heft I. Mss. Bibl. 76 u. Bibl. 22, Bamberg, 1926.

GOLDSCHMIDT ⁄ ADOLPH GOLDSCHMIDT, *Die Elfenbein⁄Skulpturen aus der Zeit der karolingischen u. sächsischen Kaiser,* Berlin, Bruno Cassirer, 1914 u. 1918.

HASELOFF, *Egb. Psalter* ⁄ HEINRICH VOLBERT SAUERLAND U. ARTHUR HASE⁄ LOFF, *Der Psalter Erzbischof Egberts von Trier* — Festschrift der Gesellschaft für nütz⁄ liche Forschungen, Trier, 1901.

HERMANN ⁄ HERM. JUL. HERMANN, *Die frühmittelalterlichen Handschriften des Abend⁄ landes* — Beschreibendes Verzeichnis der illuminierten Hss. in Oesterreich. N. F. I. (Wien Nat. Bibl.), Leipzig, 1923.

JAMES ⁄ MONTAGUE RHODES JAMES, *A Descriptive Catalogue of the Latin manuscripts in the John Rylands Library at Manchester,* Manchester, 1921.

JOSTEN, *Studien* ⁄ HANNS HEINZ JOSTEN, *Neue Studien zur Evangelienhandschrift No. 18 im Domschatz zu Hildesheim* — Studien zur deutschen Kunstgeschichte, Heft 109, Strassburg, Heitz, 1909.

KÖHLER, *Adagruppe* ⁄ WILHELM KÖHLER, *Die Tradition der Adagruppe u. die Anfänge des ottonischen Stils in der Buchmalerei* — Festschrift zum 60. Geburtstag von Paul Clemen, S. 255 ff., Düsseldorf, Schwann, 1926.

LEIDINGER, I ⁄ GEORG LEIDINGER, *Miniaturen aus Handschriften der Kgl. Hof⁄ u. Staats⁄ bibliothek in München,* Heft I. *Das sog. Evangeliarium Kaiser Ottos* III.

LEIDINGER, V ⁄ GEORG LEIDINGER, *Miniaturen aus Handschriften der Kgl. Hof⁄ u. Staatsbibliothek in München,* Heft V. *Das Perikopenbuch Kaiser Heinrichs* II.

LEIDINGER, VI ⁄ GEORG LEIDINGER, *Miniaturen aus Handschriften der Bayerischen Staatsbibliothek in München,* Heft VI. *Evangeliarium aus dem Domschatz in Bamberg.*

LEIDINGER, *Meisterwerke* ⁄ GEORG LEIDINGER, *Meisterwerke der Buchmalerei.* München, Hugo Schmidt, 1920.

LEROQUAIS ⁄ ABBÉ V. LEROQUAIS, *Les Sacramentaires et les Missels Manuscrits des Bibliothèques Publiques de France,* Paris 1924.

MERTON ⁄ ADOLF MERTON, *Die Buchmalerei in St. Gallen vom 9. bis zum 11. Jhrh.,* Leipzig, Hiersemann, 1912.

MICHEL ⁄ ANDRÉ MICHEL, *Histoire de l'Art,* I, 2, Paris, 1905.

RICHTER⁄SCHÖNFELDER ⁄ GEORG RICHTER u. ALBERT SCHÖNFELDER, *Sacramentarium Fuldense Saec. X*—Quellen u. Abhandlungen zur Geschichte der Abtei u. Diözese Fulda, IX, Fulda, 1912.

SCHMIDT ⁄ ADOLF SCHMIDT, *Die Miniaturen des Gero⁄Codex,* Leipzig, 1924.

SCHRAMM ⁄ PERCY ERNST SCHRAMM, *Zur Geschichte der Buchmalerei in der Zeit der sächsischen Kaiser*—Jahrbuch für Kunstwissenschaft, hrsg. v. Ernst Gall, I, 1923.

SWARZENSKI, I ⁄ GEORG SWARZENSKI, *Die Regensburger Buchmalerei des 10. u. 11. Jh.*—Denkmäler der süddeutschen Malerei des frühen Mittelalters, I, Leipzig, 1901.

SWARZENSKI, II ⁄ GEORG SWARZENSKI, *Die Salzburger Malerei von den ersten Anfängen bis zur Blütezeit des romanischen Stiles*—Denkmäler der süddeutschen Malerei des frühen Mittelalters, II, Leipzig, 1913.

VOEGE ⁄ WILH. VOEGE, *Eine deutsche Malerschule um die Wende des ersten Jahrtausends*—Westdeutsche Zeitschrift für Geschichte u. Kunst. Erg. Heft VII, Trier, 1891.

WEBER ⁄ LOUIS WEBER, *Einbanddecken, Elfenbeintafeln, Miniaturen, Schriftproben aus Metzer liturg. Hss.,* Metz u. Frankfurt a. M., 1912.

WÖLFFLIN ⁄ HEINRICH WÖLFFLIN, *Die Bamberger Apocalypse.* 2. Aufl. München, Kurt Wolff, 1921.

ZIMMERMANN, *Fulda* ⁄ E. HEINRICH ZIMMERMANN, *Die Fuldaer Buchmalerei in karolingischer und ottonischer Zeit* — Kunstgeschichtliches Jahrbuch der K. K. Zentralkommission zur Erhaltung u. Erforschung der Kunst⁄ u. historischen Denkmale, IV (1910), S. 1.

THE TEXT

IN his lives of the abbots of the English monastery of Weremouth the Venerable Bede relates that towards the end of the seventh century the Abbot Benedict Biscop brought from Italy picture cycles with which he decorated the walls and the ceiling of his church. The rows of pictures illustrating incidents from the Old and the New Testaments thus served to instruct and edify the people. We can, however, scarcely imagine that the abbot really brought to the North whole cart- and ship-loads of church decorations. What is more likely is that he carried with him only the models of such paintings in the form of miniatures, which were subsequently reproduced on the walls and roof. That there was no lack of talent capable of undertaking such a task is attested by the Codex Amiatinus, the manuscript of the Bible executed towards 700 in the Anglo-Saxon monastery and preserved in the Laurentian library in Florence. A further proof is furnished by the miniatures of the Evangelists in the Gospels executed at the same time at Lindisfarne after a South Italian model. To judge from the Lindisfarne Gospels, the monumental copies must have developed their own style which did not always correspond to that of the model, but the subject of the illustrations must at any rate have been clear to the spectators. Nor is the possibility excluded that, together with the models, there also came to these new centres of culture ecclesiastics trained in the South and experienced in the art of painting. What is only highly probable in regard to mural paintings becomes a certainty in the case of manuscript illuminations. Together with the sacred texts, the copyists drew from the models of early Christian and later classical art the pictorial comprehension of the narratives and the illustration of religious conceptions. That the monks must have been particularly anxious to procure such models is evident, if we remember how absolutely impossible it must have been for them to reproduce a comprehensible representation of such a rich world of incidents out of their own imagination. If we consider what a very long time classical art had taken before it had achieved an illusionistic reproduction of the world, such as has been created by Hellenistic art, we cannot help seeing that the men who had only just come into contact with

I

this culture, could not have created something similar out of their own imagination. They had only two alternatives, either to grope independently and, like children, attempt to take their first steps, or to copy as far as possible what had been done before them. They chose the latter, because the content had also been taken over from abroad. Every new model furnished new inspirations.

The first borrowings of this kind had taken place on Irish and Anglo-Saxon soil and had been afterwards united with those effected in the Carolingian Empire where, since Charlemagne, new material had been procured with great zeal. But under the Ottos, and thanks to the diligent efforts of the abbots, new material had accumulated in the scriptoria of the Eastern Frankish monasteries where the monks had already grown accustomed to artistic sumptuousness. With the renewed relations of the German Emperors with Byzantium, new sources became available. During the reigns of Charlemagne and of his successors it had been principally a question of preserving in a pure form the texts transmitted by Christian and classical tradition. For that purpose recourse was had not only to the monasteries of Monte Cassino and lower Italy, but also to the Mediterranean litoral, for frequent intercourse existed between Syria, Egypt and the other Mediterranean coasts. But under the Ottos, as it seems, the exchange of treasures between the rulers themselves began to play a more important rôle. Many a sumptuous manuscript in which particular stress was laid upon wealth of decoration and illumination, whether old or of recent execution, may thus have come to Germany.

It is rather surprising that among the manuscripts of the ninth century, we do not possess a single cycle illustrating the incidents from the New Testament, although their existence upon the walls of churches is attested by literary sources. The stories narrated in the Gospels are merely suggested, either in the initials of the Sacramentary of Drogo, dating from the time of Louis le Débonnaire, or in the shape of ornamental filling on certain decorated pages of the Gospels, or as plastic ornaments on the covers of bindings and other objects of the church. Wherever we meet with connected rows of scenes, they either relate to narratives of the Old Testament, as for instance in the Bible of St.

Paul in Rome and the Golden Psalter of St. Gall, or they illustrate scientific or edifying works, such as the Astronomy of Aratus, the *Psychomachia* of Prudentius or the comedies of Terence.

Under the Ottos the reverse was the case. Miniatures illustrating the Gospels appear in the manuscripts, while nothing concerning the narratives of the Old Testament is transmitted. Even the representations of the history of the Maccabeans in Leyden, which seem an exception, point to an older art. On the other hand, the covers of the manuscripts, instead of the multiple scenes of the Carolingian period, display rather simpler representative subjects, such as the enthroned or crucified Christ. This can scarcely be merely an accidental occurrence. The possibility of a pictorial reproduction of the New Testament existed under the Carolingians, but perhaps it was felt that the introduction of illustrations would be a disturbing element during the reading of the sacred text at ceremonies for which these books were employed. It was not until the reign of the Ottos that such scruples ceased to exist. During the latter half of the tenth century, the serious craving for culture and severe critical judgment, such as we meet in the literature of the time of Charlemagne, began to give place to a more external requirement for general world-culture, wherein aesthetic obligations played an important rôle. The fact was not without some connection with the idea of the «Roman Empire of the German nation» and an *approachment* with the Byzantine Empire.

This is therefore the time when we can speak with greater certainty of an art of illumination that is really German, without the participation of England or France: it is the moment when the German artists began to avail themselves directly of early Christian or Byzantine models, adapting or changing them to their own taste and requirements, the time when one may speak of a German art and of a German style, compared to which France during the same period produced nothing of corresponding value.

In the history of this art the most prominent place must be assigned to the scriptorium in the monastery of Reichenau, that pleasant island in the Bodensee, or Lake of Constance. Reichenau, which, as a halting place of the

Emperors on their journeys to Rome, had relations everywhere, was particularly well situated to serve as an intermediary between the South and the North. The island, which during the Carolingian period, together with St. Gall, had already been one of the foremost Alamannic centres of missionary activity, now became the seat of the Imperial chancery. It therefore stands to reason that very precious objects were preserved in the treasury of the monastery, which also became a most likely depository for Imperial gifts.

Whereas the books hitherto produced there had borne quite a various character, a new era was now suddenly inaugurated for a group of the Reichenau manuscripts. We are indebted to Wilhelm Vöge for the first critical survey of these works, and to Arthur Haseloff for their localization at Reichenau. Moreover, the kind of affinity existing between the manuscripts, and the many representations which coincide but do not give any indication of having been directly copied one from the other, lead to the conclusion of lost prototypes which had suddenly been introduced at Reichenau and become the starting point of a new artistic tendency. They stand to each other in much the relationship of texts treated in philological research for establishing the correct original.

We must also bear in mind that the monks at Reichenau were no novices in the art of drawing. Not only did they continue their former traditions, but they were also particularly capable of making independent variations and combinations. They were even able to effect a clever synthesis with important works introduced from France during an earlier period.

Just because a not inconsiderable number of illustrated manuscripts of this school has been preserved, we are able not only to get an insight into the mode of activity but also to form an idea of the cycles which underlay this work. It appears now that Reichenau possessed, about 970, two sets of illustrations. The first set consisted of a series of representations, each complete in itself, framed with a simple border. They corresponded to the later classical illustrations of Latin and Greek texts, such as the oldest manuscripts of Vergil and Homer, the Itala fragments of Quedlinburg and Byzantine manuscripts, such as the Paris Psalter Grec. 139, which point to Alexandrian models. The second set consisted of continuous narratives in bands, either in the form of scrolls or transferred to the pages of a codex in a series of rows. We meet the reproductions of this set in Carolingian manuscripts, in the Bibles of Tours, in the Byzantine Gregory of Nazianzus in Paris, and traces of it in the Vienna Genesis. The monks of Reichenau chose their models from both sets, and the original style is frequently reflected in their borrowings. The difference is already evident in the two oldest productions, the Gospels written for Otto II or III and preserved in the Cathedral of Aix-la-Chapelle (Plates 1-3), and the Pericopes executed for Archbishop Egbert of Trèves and written, probably about 980, by Kerald and Heribert, two monks of Reichenau (Plates 4-6). Of these two manuscripts, the latter is in its essence derived from the first source. It displays not only picture-like scenes, framed in a narrow border embellished only with a gilt chain of lozenges, and with an illusionistic tinted background, but also a number of figures and groups very closely related to classical art in their pictorial execution. On the contrary, the Codex of Aix-la-Chapelle seems to point more to a continuous series. This is seen in the detached single groups, complementing each other in the narrative and painted on a purple ground. This is also confirmed by the fact that, with few exceptions, scenes which mostly correspond with it in the Bamberg Gospels of Otto (Munich, Cod. 4453, Cim. 58) (Plates 24-29), also seem to indicate derivation from a continuous series, in spite of a different arrangement. A further comparison, however, of the Munich and Aix-la-Chapelle Gospels shows that the former is not a copy of the latter, but that both codices can be traced to a common model. Whereas, however, the Aix-la-Chapelle Gospels imitated more closely the richer execution of groups and the more natural movements of that model, the Munich Codex displays a diminution. On the other hand the latter manuscript has copied from its model figures which could find no room in the Aix-la-Chapelle Codex. This is due to the fact that Liuthar, the illuminator of the latter manuscript, on account of the narrow tall shape and the insertion in the arcaded frame, was compelled either to shorten the scenes as far as possible or to place them one above the other. Whenever such a proceeding proved impracticable, as is the case in the scene of the Crucifixion with the thieves (Plate 3), the figures get into the border. Wherever again the illuminator was satisfied with one single scene, he either raised the architectural designs of the background to an unusual height or repeated the secondary figures in two rows one above the other. The notion of the series of scenes in the model is further strengthened by representations found in the Munich Lectionary (Clm. 23338) (Plate 34), due no doubt to the same artist's hand. The painter, however, did not limit himself to one source. On the contrary, the last miniatures of the Munich Gospels show that the Codex Egberti had also served as a model. This becomes clear from the similar compositions in both codices and the introduction of an illusionistic sky background in place of purple or gold. The frame, composed of a chain of lozenges has also been taken over, but in all this it is evidently not the Codex Egberti itself which served as a model, but another common prototype. On the other hand, the illuminators of the Codex Egberti seem themselves not only to have drawn from this model, but to have borrowed occasionally from the other continuous series. Such a combination of different models particularly prevailed in the execution of the portraits of the Evangelists which always precede their Gospels. They are chosen from among the great number of types handed down by the Carolingian period, rather than from new sources. The illuminators of these manuscripts naturally tried above all to imitate the style of their models, as is specially the case in the composition of the scenes. Nevertheless, the skill and capacity of the artists and also their striving for adaptation were not of the same degree. The Codex Egberti displays the work of three different hands, one of which is clearly reminiscent of and approaches the classical style of painting. This is evident in the broad pictorial reproduction of the large heads, in the free spatial difference in the position of the feet as well as in the loose grouping of crowds of figures (Plates 4 B). However, in other pictures the figures are all placed in a row on the lower border of the frame, the heads of the groups are fitted into fixed horizontal lines, while faces and the

6

cast of drapery are harder and more in accordance with the rules of drawing handed down from the Ada School (Plate 6B).

In colouring, all these miniatures display greater power in the light, brighter and more joyful gradations of colour than are exhibited in the variegated but dull and heavy miniatures of the Carolingian period, in particular those of the Ada group. The beauty, therefore, of the best works produced in the scriptorium of Reichenau, being the first that followed the newly transmitted models, consists in a noble balancing of the composition and in a restrained use of line, both inheritances taken over from the model. But the impulse innate in the Northerners soon led to other goals.

To the above mentioned group, which in its manner is still closely allied to the antique, belong, in addition to the Codex Egberti, the Chantilly Sacramentary from Lorsch (Plate 12), the Registrum Gregorii at Trèves (Plate 7), the imperial miniature of which is preserved at Chantilly (Plate 8), the Gospels of the Sainte Chapelle in Paris, Lat. 8851 (Plates 9-11 and 16A), the Paris Sacramentary, Lat. 10501 (Plate 15), a manuscript of the Gospels in the monastery of Strahow at Prague (Plate 13A), and others.

It must now be remembered that the Codex Egberti was executed for Trèves and probably presented to the local monastery of St. Paulinus by the archbishop, that the closely allied Berlin Epistolary was also written for St. Paulinus, and that lastly, both the Registrum Gregorii and the Paris manuscript Lat. 10501 equally point to Trèves. For all these reasons it is highly possible that one of the illuminators of the Codex Egberti, probably the one who added the first pictures, had emigrated to Trèves, where he continued to paint in his own style or to teach others. The above mentioned series of manuscripts, although emanating from Reichenau, may therefore have been executed not on the island but in Trèves. Such is also the opinion of Haseloff.

This entire group, which may presumably be localized in Trèves, is distinguished by a noble repose. The outlines are drawn in long even curves, the modelling is effected in smooth rotundity, without any energetic contrasts in light and shade, while the colours, in harmony with it, produce a light, even

7

pallid effect. The gestures are reserved, and the expression of the heads is without any strong movement but of quiet beauty. The architectural designs, too, show a certain purity of line and a comparatively correct perspective. To this is added a balance in the composition which is similarly expressed in the more lively scenes in the Codex Egberti. All these qualities show the classical tendencies and inspiration of Greek models, although they are not perfectly similar. On the contrary, the style betrays an independent artistic personality, the product of the new age.

This personality, however, does not fully represent the new artistic generation in Germany, which was striving after a stronger dynamic expression and preferred rich ornamental values to a quiet optical reality. Against such a temperament, which must have begun to stir as soon as the means had to a certain extent been mastered, the style of adaptation could hardly prevail either here or in any other German art centre.

Thus the Aix-la-Chapelle Gospels already manifest an inclination towards a transformation of the organic connection of objects, as seen, into an arbitrary collocation of separate elements. This new tendency is shown in the more elongated figures, in the tense spreading out of some of the ends of the drapery, and in the precision and independence displayed in separating and encircling the details of body or drapery.

This process, which with all its consequences can be followed in Reichenau itself, leads to those manuscripts which are to be considered as an indigenous artistic creation. The best known and most sumptuous of such books, is the Gospels of Otto III, Clm. 4453. In addition to the dedication page, the miniatures of the Evangelists and the canon-tables, it contains numerous representations illustrating events from the Gospels (Plates 24-29). As this manuscript has many compositions in common with the older Aix-la-Chapelle one, the following point deserves particular notice: the outlines are simplified, thus making the movements of the figures appear harsher. The result, however, is not increased precision of illustration, but, on the contrary, an impoverishment of natural form in favour of the accentuation

8

of firmly defined lines, an accentuation which is still more strengthened by the addition of tense drapery ends or ray-like folds.

In the miniature of the enthroned Emperor (Plate 24 B), the acute-angled drapery folds directed downward and the position of the arm harmonize with the sweeps of the curtain which is looped back, while the roof and gables are framed by a symmetrical outline that disregards spatial correctness. The lance-bearer is to be imagined as standing behind the Protospatarius, although his round shield lies in front of him. The provinces which are paying homage are schematically repeating the movements of both striding and bowing. Everything tends toward ornamental rhythm and distinctly drawn lines.

It was not for the first time, however, that this manner was adopted. Such an accentuation of linear drawing had really been inaugurated in another group of manuscripts coming from Reichenau. The execution of these had started several decades earlier, following an older German inheritance. Continuing a process which had originated with the Carolingian group of the Ada manuscript (see Vol. I), this style permeated with its ferment the new pictorial productions of Reichenau so that the latter began to display a tendency in a similar direction.

In the forefront of that older series stands the Sacramentary (Plates 17 and 18) executed at Reichenau for Archbishop Gero before he had assumed his episcopal dignity in 969. The manuscript is a close imitation of another belonging to the Ada group and is most closely related to the Rome-Karlsburg Gospels which are a century older (Plate 18 B). This applies also to the Petershausen Sacramentary (Plate 19) which has been proved to be closely connected with Reichenau. Allied to these manuscripts is the Psalter of Archbishop Egbert of Trèves (977-993) at Cividale (Plates 20 and 21). The style of this manuscript, written by one Ruodprecht, exhibits a stronger ornamental manner. An extraordinary wealth of decorative elements enlivens the background with birds and fantastic quadrupeds, painted in gold on a purple ground and reminiscent in their technical execution of the Ada group, or completely covers the ground with texture patterns and harmonises with the luxuriant plait-and tendril-work of the initials influenced perhaps by St. Gall, and the firm bands of light and shade of the drapery folds, as is particularly noticeable in the dedication page (Plates 19 and 20).

The manner, too, of expressing the lights by means of lines and strokes is already clearly displayed in the Ada group and there is no doubt that it is ultimately to be traced to Eastern models. It is a manner frequently used in Byzantine productions, particularly in connection with an application of gold, and was practised down to a later period. Closely allied to the Cividale Psalter, perhaps even the work of the same illuminator, are the Gospels of Poussay (Plate 22).

That the Codex Egberti of Trèves, though executed in quite a different manner, is still allied to the productions of Ruodprecht is shown by the representation of the adoration of the Magi (Plate 6 B) in the former, where the illuminator tries to imitate that style. A certain combination with the pictorial manner is also evident in the Hornbach Sacramentary, written by the scribe Eburnant (Plate 23), to whom the Liuthar group in its first productions, such as the Gospels of Aix-la-Chapelle (Plates 1-3) and the Codex Egberti, must already have been known.

At about the same time as the manuscripts of the Liuthar group, and perhaps by the same illuminator, were executed the Josephus manuscript at Bamberg and the Lectionary at Munich (Clm. 23338) (Plate 34).

Besides these, the two handsome Bamberg manuscripts, the Commentary on Isaiah (Plate 30) and the Daniel Commentary (Plate 31) are very closely allied and exhibit a particularly fine decorative quality.

A further step away from classical tradition is taken in the book of Pericopes (Clm. 57), written between 1002 and 1014 for Henry II and his wife, and presented by the Emperor as a gift to the cathedral of Bamberg (Plates 35-37). As for the Bamberg Apocalypse (Plate 39), written by the same hand, it had probably already been executed during the last years of the reign of Otto III and taken over by Henry. In many miniatures the book of Pericopes follows the Gospels of Otto, but it also reproduces many scenes not found in the latter and which must probably be traced to the common first source. There is, however, a fundamental change of style, chiefly consisting in a greater freedom of the lines now enclosing the flat forms in the long drawn curves. In addition to this, we notice three sharply defined and uniformly col-oured bands instead of the backgrounds with coloured sky. The conception of space is thus completely given up.

The linear style is even further increased in a manuscript of the Gospels written ten years later and which is also one of the gifts offered by Henry to Bamberg Cathedral (Clm. 4454, Cim. 59) (Plates 38 B, 40). In this manuscript the movement of the line strokes becomes even more abrupt and vehement, as they suddenly break up and reverse their direction. The figures of the Evangelists consequently give the impression of the highest excitement.

The psychological tenor of these men can scarcely be distinguished from the ornamental character. In the imagination of the draughtsman both evi-dently coincided. This is clearly reflected in the ornamentation where the growing tendrils in the initials and in the decorated pages of this last manu-script convey, in the change of their directions, the impression of leaping and jumping. The shoots, breaking up sharply and in an angular direction, dart out and spread widely (Plate 38), whereas originally the tendency to the centrifugal was indicated only by arrow-like leaves branching out from the quiet, band-like intertwistings and spirals, to which the addition of round buds lent the appearance of plants. The luxurious growth of the branches gradually followed the same manner, and by its motion it lent to the vegetation an aspect of capricious energy.

The most eloquent proof of the connection existing between the ornamen-tal element and a tendency to expression is furnished by the miniatures of the Evangelists in the manuscript of the Munich Gospels Cim. 58 (Plates 25 and 26). Here, as in a vision, the Saint with an ecstatic gaze is surrounded by prophets and angels who are made subservient to his appearance by means of united circles representing the highest emanation of his being. Rays ra-

11

diate from them like fireworks in all directions and convey the impression of a momentary explosion, while below flows peacefully the river of salvation out of which the believers or their symbols are drinking.

Such representations are repeated with great partiality in the Bamberg Commentary on Isaiah (Plate 30), in the Roman Gospels (Plate 32) and also in the Ansfried Gospels at Utrecht.

The influence of the school of Reichenau radiated and extended far and wide. On the one hand, manuscripts were executed at Reichenau for foreign personages, such as Gero and Hillinus of Cologne and Egbert of Trèves, not to count temporal princes and rulers. On the other hand, itinerant monks carried the pictorial art of Reichenau to other monasteries where they con-tinued it, sometimes inaugurating the artistic activity, or effecting a fusion with the indigenous style. Thus a series of manuscripts was executed at Min-den under Abbot Sigebert (1022-1036) which may be considered as derived from Reichenau. The penetration of elements from Reichenau is further evi-dent at Ratisbon and other Bavarian schools, while in Cologne and Fulda and as far as Bremen, there were signs of a style which had undoubtedly o-riginated at Reichenau. This is above all to be explained by the fact that Rei-chenau had inaugurated a style which best met the requirements of the gener-al artistic sentiments and feelings of the period.

The style of the Reichenau-Trèves school is continued in the monastery of Echternach whither the imperial Chancery had been transferred. The artis-tic activity was introduced, fostered and developed thanks to the efforts of Archbishop Egbert, but it flourished and reached its climax only under Henry III (1039-1056).

The starting point of the Echternach school of painting is the sumptuous codex of the Gospels written in the years 983-991 for the youthful Otto III and his mother Theophano. The manuscript is now preserved at Gotha and, on account of its golden letters, is known as the Codex Aureus Epterna-censis (Plates 43-49). Whether the manuscript was really executed in Ech-ternach or in the then more important neighbouring centre of Trèves, is not absolutely certain. At any rate, it differs unmistakably in style from the productions executed at Reichenau and Trèves, and all its offshoots are to be found in Echternach, a monastery reorganised since 974.

Although a new style must naturally be the creation of a prominent personality and cannot emanate from the ambient void, the name of the artist who illuminated the Codex Aureus is unknown. The illuminator shows a close connection with the artist of the Trèves manuscripts, the Registrum Gregorii and the Gospels of the Sainte Chapelle. The miniatures of the Evangelists in the Codex Aureus show that this codex, like the latter manuscripts, had received its strongest stimulus from the work of the Ada group, which it resembles in the entire arrangement. On the other hand, deviation from the Ada group, in the same way as in the work of the Gregory master, is shown by a greater simplicity and smoothness of the lines and the colours which betray a significant independence of that older school. The difference of style, however, between the Codex Aureus and the Gregory master becomes particularly evident when we compare the two Majestas miniatures in the manuscripts of the Sainte Chapelle (Plate 9) and Gotha (Plate 43) respectively. These miniatures resemble each other so closely in their arrangement, that we can only assume that one artist had copied from the other, unless both had before them a common model. But in the first place the Echternach manuscript exhibits a difference in the types of the heads. Instead of the usual youthful, beardless type, this manuscript shows heads with long pointed beards, not only in the corner circles, where they represent prophets instead of apostles, but also in all the other miniatures. The heads are further distinguished by an extraordinarily low forehead and by an enormous bony nose, which, in the later manuscripts of Echternach, becomes strikingly ugly. Above all, the movement of the outlines has a more lively aspect. The compactness of the figure of Christ in the Gospels of the Sainte Chapelle is destroyed in the Gotha manuscript by the fact that the right hand in the gesture of blessing is raised higher, while the hand holding the book is moved to the side, and the knees are wider apart. A certain degree of excitement is also noticeable in the way in which one foot of the prophets is lifted up on its toes and retreats farther back, while the hands are stretched more forward. The symbols of the Evangelists are also twisted and curved. The ornamental elements increase, the spikes of the circular frames, the details of the wings, the decorative stripes in the drapery and all the lines tend toward a stronger, more powerful expression. We notice here a tendency similar to that which influenced the change in the Bamberg manuscripts of Reichenau. The Codex Aureus therefore, compared to the Gospels of the Sainte Chapelle, must be considered as the later production.

While the figures have now completely abandoned the oriental element, which still prevailed in the miniatures of the Evangelists in the Ada group, particularly with regard to technical execution, new influences from Byzantium make themselves felt. They were the result of a closer intercourse between the imperial house and the Greek capital, and met the ornamental requirement rather than affected the modelling of the figures. Decorated full pages now appear, imitating Sassanid-Byzantine textiles (Plate 48). The marriage deed of Otto II and Theophano, still preserved in the archives of Wolfenbüttel, was written upon a background which gave the impression of such a purple fabric with animal designs. In a lesser degree this is also evident in the Reichenau manuscripts which besides introduce the Byzantine floral forms for decorating the initials and borders (Plate 42). These patterned backgrounds were of the greatest importance for the book decoration of the future, not only on account of the fact that this element spread all over Germany, penetrating particularly the Saxon districts, but also because it constituted the introduction of an independant treatment of the background, which created its own patterns, and affected to a high degree the depthlessness of the miniatures. This is in accordance with the general anticlassical mediaeval tendency which consisted in concentrating the figure scenes in one plane and in laying stress upon the drawing of the outline by means of a carpet-like background. With a patterned ground the depth of space for the figures is not only cut off but the figure itself is set off from its surroundings, while the decorative nature of the miniatures is heightened. The later Romanesque period emancipated itself from this manner, and it was only during the Gothic period that a new form of a patterned ground had set in. There, however, it only served the purpose of separating the figures plastically.

In the ornamentation of the initials the Echternach style resembles that of Reichenau in the tendril-like plait-work with shooting buds. Instead, however, of imitating the leaping, angular motion of the Liuthar group, the ornamentation is composed of quieter spirals and rounded branchlets (Plate 49). The manuscripts caused to be executed by the imperial family are generally of a very large size, but there are also some comparatively small, although not less rich in miniatures, such as the manuscripts in Bremen and Brussels.

The connection existing between the Codex Aureus of Echternach and the manuscripts of Trèves has already been explained. Barring a few insignificant alterations, the miniatures of the Evangelists as well as the Majestas in the former, were copied from the Gospels of the Sainte Chapelle. On the other hand, hardly any scenes from the Gospels are allied with those in the Codex Egberti, while the narratives in the Bremen manuscript (Plates 52-55) resemble them so exactly, that they must be an imitation either of the latter or of a common model, whereas the parables in it are taken from those in the Gotha manuscript. The narrative illustrations repeated in the Brussels manuscript (Plate 56) are also closely related. The rich architectural crestings which appear in isolated instances and which we also meet in the miniatures of the legend of St. Stephen in the Brussels codex, may be a free addition by the hand of the illuminator of Echternach. Sometimes he is stirred by a desire to panel out the space in ornamental compartments, as we shall notice later on in the productions of Ratisbon, and as it is clearly seen in the scenes of the Annunciation and the birth of Christ in the Gospels of Luxeuil, a Paris manuscript from Echternach (Plate 51).

Compared with the works coming from Trèves, executed in a more pictorial and smoother style, the Echternach manuscripts are harsher in their outlines and in their separations of the parts as well as in the modelling. The large heads are vaguely reminiscent of the middle Byzantine average type of masculine head. As for the relations with Greece, it is significant that the Greek inscriptions accompanying the pictorial miniatures of Trèves, such as those found in the Gospels of the Sainte Chapelle and in the Lorsch Sacramentary at Chantilly, are really Greek texts, whereas the Echternach manuscripts mostly exhibit Latin captions written with Greek letters, often wrongly employed. The Ottonian Codex Aureus remained for a long time the criterion for Echternach, and although the number of Biblical scenes represented in this school is more considerable than in any other contemporary scriptorium, the variety of invention is small indeed. Fifty years elapse between the execution of the Gotha Codex, written in the tenth century, and the next dated production. It still, however, remains for future research to ascertain how many of the other manuscripts, as for instance the Gospels of Luxeuil (Plates 50 and 51), which, to judge by their style, belong here, are to be placed in the intervening period. The most sumptuous illuminated codices are gifts of Henry III, the first of them being the Pericopes at Bremen (Plates 52-55), completed before the Emperor's marriage with Agnes. In style, this manuscript greatly resembles the Codex Egberti whose miniatures it mostly copies, whereas the Brussels Codex which, as it seems, was also destined for Bremen, exhibits this influence in a lesser degree (Plate 56). Gisela, the pious widow of Conrad II, was the patroness of Bremen, and she also figures in the Bremen manuscript with equal right by the side of her son. The latter dedicated to her, as well as to his father, a pious memorial in the large manuscript of the Escorial (50 cm x 35 cm.) (Plates 57-62). On the first page the imperial parents are represented as kneeling before the enthroned Christ (Plate 57), whereas, on the next page, Henry III himself and his wife Agnes are paying homage to the Virgin (Plate 58). The Gospels, a gift offered to the cathedral of Speyer, built by Conrad, were not, as has often been assumed, executed during the lifetime of this Emperor, but between the years 1043 and 1046, as is irrefutably proved by the various inscriptions. This manuscript with more than fifty illustrations and numerous decorated pages, perfectly preserved, constitutes one of the most important monuments of German painting of the eleventh century. Next to this in date come the Gospels offered as a gift to the cathedral of Goslar and executed after Henry's coronation in 1046, probably for the dedication of the cathedral in 1050. They are now preserved in the University Library of Upsala (Plates 63-66). This manuscript exhibits already the tendency of the middle of the century towards schematic parallel lines, but in all other respects it still displays the specific type of Echternach. The style remained vivid until the end of the century, finding its last representation in the Life of St. Willibrord by Theofreid, of 1105, now preserved at Gotha.

Dependent upon Echternach are also the works of the neighbouring monastery of Prüm. An Antiphonary of a very narrow oblong shape, executed there, is in Paris (Plate 68), and a Lectionary is in the Rylands Library in Manchester (Plates 69-71). The style of the former manuscript, written about 990, although somehow allied to the book of Pericopes of Echternach, which is preserved in Brussels, is nevertheless different from it, and reminiscent of French Carolingian works. The second manuscript coincides iconographically with the Echternach productions, but it displays a remarkably watered style, and a dilution and an attenuation both in the widely drawn out compositions as well as in the very light colours and the thinness of the impasto. Nevertheless, the fine and modest, though schematic, drawing is not without artistic charm (Plates 69,70 and 71).

It was with a view to an ornamental decoration of the page that the illuminators liked to panel out the big space, either into single compartments or into a border and a middle square. This square was again subdivided, while the border was separated into single compartments, corner and central squares. Such separations not only constituted right angles, but diagonal, rhombic and round compartments being added, they formed triangles and spandrels. Such a system of panels and compartments, which emanated from a mere ornamental instinct and was filled with decorative patterns and designs,

17

we meet earlier in illuminations produced on Irish and Anglo-Saxon soil. Frequently figure designs are also employed to fill out the compartments, such as the emblems of the Evangelists and Christian symbols, or the Hand of God and the dove. The Carolingian scriptoria had adopted these patterns and carried them beyond the Rhine to the East.

The visionary miniatures of the Evangelists in the Gospels of Otto III are the result of such a panelling out of the space into compartments. The pattern, however, was not a device perceived merely externally, but was also inspired by spiritual and dogmatic relations. A spiritual structure corresponded to the ornamental arrangement, giving expression to the relations between the Old Testament figures, the prophets and angels, and the Evangelists and their emblems. The device is a mediaeval creation, which later on entered into the the systems of the Biblia Pauperum and similar cycles. It found a particular scope under the Saxon Emperor Henry II at Ratisbon, where the illuminations of the Codex Aureus of Charles the Bald in the monastery of St. Emmeram inspired such divisions. Whereas the Sacramentary of Henry II (Plates 72-75) only imitated Carolingian manuscripts, the Gospels produced by this Emperor, and now preserved in the Vatican (Plate 78), proceed in an independent manner. It is above all the Gospels of Uota of Niedermünster (Plates 76 and 77) which form the climax with their ornamental and complicated compartments of a Biblical and mystical tenor.

In many respects the Sacramentary of Henry II is closely allied to the Codex Aureus of Charles the Bald which was probably executed in St. Denis about 870 and presumably brought to Ratisbon by Arnulf of Kärnthen. The Sacramentary drew many an inspiration from the latter manuscript, particularly from its rich ornamental motives, and endeavoured to produce similar effects by means of numerous white high lights on the borders of the leafwork. The repetition, however, of illustrations from the Carolingian codex is not limited to decorated pages, but extends also to the miniatures. Thus the miniature of Henry (Plate 73) is simply a copy of the enthroned Charles the Bald. It is just this agreement between the two manuscripts which helps us

18

to distinguish quite clearly the difference existing between the two centuries. First of all, the technical execution of the Ottonian manuscript is of a different character, entirely Byzantine. The artist, presumably not really a Greek, had undoubtedly received Greek training. He thus lays on the ground-colour of the flesh in a green tint and then proceeds with his modelling, producing the light with a reddish yellow tint merging into white. In the drawing of the features, too, the choice of brown, red and green frequently coincides with the Oriental-Byzantine scheme which we already know from the Ada group. In the Carolingian model, on the other hand, the modelling is effected loosely with only reddish brown, and the features are also tinted in a brown tone. The execution in the latter manuscript is also throughout much softer and more pictorial, whereas in the Sacramentary of Henry it is sharper and more precise; the shading is gradual and in several places provided with a black outline. Reminiscent of the Byzantine manner are the sharply inserted angular lights in the drapery folds and, above all, the type of the features, the aquiline nose, with the triangular form on the top, and the broad skull. Although details of such an eastern influence had already manifested themselves in the Rule of Niedermünster, executed in Ratisbon about 990, the teaching received from Byzantium now appears here for the first time in all its vigour.

At the same time the local stylistic tendency makes itself felt in a preference for flatness and a strong variety of tints. Whereas in the Carolingian manuscript of the Gospels the figures stand in front of a real wall in the background, casting their shadows upon it, in the Sacramentary, an unreal ornamental background extends behind the whole picture. The side cupolas and spires in the space become flat rounded arches, while the figures, unlike those of the Gospels, seem to be soaring in the air instead of standing upon firm ground. Furthermore, in the Gospels, with the exception of Charles the Bald, arrayed in blue and purple robes, all the draperies exhibit a white or a reddish brown tint, and the entire picture is heightened by gold lights which soften down the colours, whereas in the Sacramentary of Henry green, blue, red and violet constantly alternate. Darker nuances indicate the shading, while the lights are expressed in lighter colours, and sometimes also in other tones, as yellow and green. The dress of Henry is also more richly decorated, so that both the distinctly ornamental character and the wider deviation from an illusionistic ideal are unmistakable. The same style is also exhibited in the coronation of Henry by Christ (Plate 72) and in the miniatures of the writing Gregory (Plate 74) and of the Maries at the tomb. On the other hand, a different style, both in drawing and painting, is displayed in the scene of the Crucifixion (Plate 75), thus betraying the hand of another artist. Although many details have been borrowed from the Byzantine manner, as is evident in the green ground colours, in the head and the loin-cloth of the crucifix, and in the misunderstood Greek inscription, a tendency, similar to that of Reichenau, is prevalent. It consists in a preference for a separation of the drapery motives by means of sharp lines and in a flat colouring without gradual modelling. Thus a new manner is adopted which becomes authoritative for a future Bavarian artistic style. The influence of Reichenau or Trèves, as it is also displayed in the small secondary scenes of the Uota manuscript will no doubt have contributed to the development of this manner. The Byzantine patterns continue in their further assimilation, particularly in the Bavarian and Salzburg monasteries of the eleventh century, until they are renewed and strengthened in the twelfth century. It was at the monastery of Seeon that the Gospels of Henry in the library of Bamberg (Plate 79) were executed. They belong to the same Germanized style as the Crucifixion in the Ratisbon Sacramentary, although exhibiting a somewhat weaker temperament and a very thin watery colouring. Compared with the productions directly derived from the Reichenau school, such a Bavarian-Austrian group constituted during the second half of the eleventh century a parallel production of illustrations, although, in many respects different and more long lived. Among the earlier productions of this style, the Gospels of the Abbess Uota of Niedermünster (1002-1025) are the most thoroughly executed and in themselves uniform and complete. They not only display the highest as-

surance in the drawing but also the greatest wealth in the ornamental panelling into various compartments (Plates 76 and 77). The leafwork, which
still retains much from the Gospels of Charles the Bald in St. Emmeram,
stands in complete harmony with the letters in the inscriptions, the large and
small figures, the busts and scenes. The desire for decorative appearance as
well as spiritual edification is thoroughly gratified, as a great deal of theological learning and erudition is interwoven with the artistic motives. Closely allied with the Uota Gospels, although more simple in their tenor, are
the miniatures in the Gospels of Henry II in Rome (Plate 78).

A certain connection evidently exists between the manifestations of style
and the political conceptions of the time. The imperial idea of Charlemagne
having once more come to the front under the Ottos, the manuscripts produced at the instigation of the Saxon Emperors reach back to the sumptuous
imperial productions of Charlemagne and his immediate successors, whereas
the period from the last decades of the ninth century to the middle of the tenth
had shown a poverty in sumptuous productions. We notice a similar proceeding in various other centres. In Reichenau, Trèves and Fulda the Gospels
of the Ada group are once more taken up, at Ratisbon the Codex Aureus of
Charles the Bald is imitated, while in Cologne the illuminators are guided
by the decorative manner of the school which took its inception from the
Gospels in the Vienna Schatzkammer. Already during the Carolingian period, these manuscripts had exercised their influence upon Franco-Saxon
painting, and their style, allied to insular ornamental motives, also effected
its entry into Cologne. Nevertheless, the Cologne illuminators must also have
had before their eyes productions of a purer style emanating from the Palace
School, perhaps from the neighbouring Aix-la-Chapelle. Cologne may thus
be considered as a centre where several sources met and mingled, and where
also the influence exercised by the Reichenau manuscripts was felt. It was,
however, the Palace School that was the standard for the Cologne productions, lending them their peculiar character and thus accentuating from early
times a tendency to illusionistic conception and style. Even at later periods

these characteristics distinguished the productions of the Lower Rhine from those of Southern Germany. The series of manuscripts which is still extant is opened by the Lectionary of Archbishop Evergerus of Cologne (985-999) who, in an attitude of worship before the Apostles, opens the text (Plate 80). The archbishop is lying flat on the ground, instead of kneeling with body bent forward as is the fashion in the Byzantine manner of worship. Compared with the painting of Trèves and Reichenau, the light tints are laid on loosely and unevenly and are not bordered by any firm outline. The drawing of the faces displays a pictorial character, and scarcely indicates the shadowless lower eye-lid. There is no trace of the schematic alternation of colours in the production of the face drawing as we find it in the Ada group and the manuscripts inspired by its style. The somewhat faulty Greek inscriptions indicating the names point at least to a certain appreciation of Greek, and the question arises as to what extent both here and in the following productions Greek models had served as a standard. The latter need not have existed in their original form, but in such as they had been transmitted by the Palace School, which had presumably drawn inspiration from the Byzantine Renaissance. The models of the Palace School may also have contained, in addition to the miniatures of the Evangelists, scenes from the Gospels which have not been preserved.

In one of the standard Cologne manuscripts, such as the Paris Sacramentary Cod. Lat. 817 (Plate 81), palpable borrowing from Byzantine iconography is evident. This occurs in the Crucifixion where the incomprehensible background of hills behind St. John and St. Mary recall to mind the illustrations found in eastern representations, as in the crucifixion of Sta. Maria Antiqua at Rome in the eighth century. Such also are the angel at the sepulchre after the Resurrection and the groups in the scenes of the Ascension and the Pentecost. At the same time, however, we find unfamiliar traits and also compositions which we only meet in Carolingian art, so that we can scarcely imagine the influence of a model reaching back to the early Christian period. The scenic accessories of this workshop increase considerably in the Gospels of the Abbess Hitda of the abbey of Meschede in Westphalia, a book which is preserved at Darmstadt (Plates 86 and 87). It contains scenes from the youth of Christ and a whole series of miracles which in addition to Byzantine manner in the formation of groups are, as the Baptism of Christ and the miracle of the Storm (Plate 87), inspired by an illusionism unknown in other manuscripts of the time. The elaborate landscapes inserted in the majority of the pictures, so extended as hardly to find room by the side of the figures, can scarcely be imagined as having been painted except from a naturalistic model. As for the provenance of such models, it is made clear by the Evangelists in the Gospels which also come from St. Gereon in Cologne and are preserved in the Municipal Archives there (Nr. 313) (Plate 82). The miniatures agree entirely with those contained in the Gospels of the Vienna Schatzkammer, emanating from the so-called Palace School (Vol. I, Plate 22). Here we also possess the source of the pictorial-illusionistic style displayed not only in the above named manuscript, but also in such others as the Gospels in Milan (Plates 83 and 84 A), in Stuttgart (Plates 88, 89 and 90 A), in Giessen (Plates 84 B and 85), in Gerresheim and in Darmstadt (Plate 90 B). It is quite possible, as we have already pointed out, that the Palace School which presumably had its seat at Aix-la-Chapelle, possessed a cycle of Biblical scenes which has been lost. In such a case, however, like the Vienna miniatures of the Evangelists, the cycle must have originated in the classical Renaissance at Byzantium, after the iconoclastic controversy.

All these Cologne manuscripts are connected by style and technique and differ entirely from the productions of Reichenau and Trèves. The colours in works of this school are not uniformly laid on and neatly separated, but exhibit a gradation of darker and lighter tones which either merge one into the other or appear suddenly, producing a reflex impression. The strong high lights frequently laid on in white patches, in addition to a technical execution of thickly applied colours and a frequently shiny surface, lend to the picture very realistic optical character, as compared to the style of the Liuthar group of Reichenau, which is expressed in lines and flat and quiet tones.

To this must be added the darker and heavier colouring of the Cologne, manuscripts. A purple violet tone prevails not only in the ground colour modelled by darker gradations of the same tint and containing a darkish drawing of the features, but also in many other parts of the picture of dark blue colour or nuances derived from a violet tint. On the whole, green and yellow tints are much less used than the others, so that the gloomy impression of the colouring forms a strong contrast to the glaring lights. The background, on account of its many landscape elements, heightens the illusionistic impression. The landscape is more profusely exhibited in the Hitda codex, whereas in the other manuscripts it shrinks to coloured stripes, swelling or decreasing, and upon which are more or less clearly indicated the earth, rows of plants and the passage of clouds.

Another point that this group has in common with the productions of the Palace School is the great simplicity of the frame, sometimes surmounted by a gable. From the Palace School is also borrowed the representation of the Evangelists as authors without their appropriate symbols, in contradistinction to other Carolingian groups.

That relations existed between Cologne and Reichenau is not only proved by the fact that monks migrated from this monastery to Cologne, but is also attested by the Gospels, written for Cologne at the request of Abbot Hillinus, and still preserved in the Cathedral, and which fits into the frame of the Liuthar group of Reichenau. Pursuing still further the Cologne manuscripts, we notice a change of the pictorial style into a more pronouncedly linear, Alamannic manner. The former compositions are retained, but the details of the drapery are more sharply separated, so that the linear arrangement stands out more clearly, while the modelling becomes harsher and more schematic. At the same time, the colouring becomes rather richer and more variegated, and the background is laid on with gold. This alteration has affected the manuscripts in the Ecclesiastical Seminary at Cologne (Plate 91), in Bamberg (Plates 92 and 93) and in Stuttgart (Plate 94), but it is not solely to be considered as a consequence of the influence of Reichenau. Cologne therein followed the general tendency of the age which consisted in developing a linear ornamental style instead of a spatial and illusionistic one. This tendency was considerably strengthened, when the modelling was reduced to the lowest terms, and the drawing of the lines to the greatest simplicity, accentuated by a parallel direction. The ornamental structure thus completely dominates the figure, but just because of this fact it produces a peculiar aesthetic impression. This is evident in a manuscript coming from St. Gereon at Cologne and preserved at Stuttgart (Plate 94), which imitates the more pictorial corresponding Gospels of the same church (Plate 82). This is even more clearly displayed in manuscripts preserved in Berlin and coming from the church of Abdinghof near Paderborn (Plates 95 and 96A), in London (Brit. Mus. Harl. 2820) coming from St. Gereon at Cologne, in Fribourg (Plate 96B), and in many others.

Of all these Cologne manuscripts none are dated, but their relative sequence may be gathered in its essence from the corresponding development of the style exhibited in them, which probably extends over the period from 1000 to 1060.

It was probably Cologne which provided the Northern German maritime districts with manuscripts. Thus, according to the pericopes, the Gospels now preserved in the Provincial Museum at Hannover were destined for St. Peter's Cathedral in Bremen. This manuscript exhibits in its light and dark drapery a treatment similar to that of the last Cologne group, but is executed by an artist trained in the Reichenau style. He may either have migrated to Cologne or been active somewhere else, perhaps in Bremen itself, where the influences of both Cologne and Reichenau were combined. Such is also the case with a manuscript of the Gospels in Munich (Plate 97) which, on account of the stress laid upon St. Willehad, points to Bremen. This manuscript is somewhat less removed from the pictorial style, and exhibits the iconographical peculiarity that in the miniatures of the Evangelists, in addition to the symbol, also the dove of the Holy Ghost inspires the author. A similar exception is displayed in a manuscript of the Gospels in the Rylands

Library in Manchester (Plate 98) which, though different in style, seems to have been written either for Bremen or Hamburg, to judge from the stress laid upon St. Ansgarius in its pericopes. On the other hand, the symbols of the Evangelists placed in a medallion point to the Franco-Saxon school whose influence effected its entry particularly by way of Cologne.

It is perhaps by the same path, that have come the corresponding characteristics in the Hildesheim manuscripts (Plates 99-105). In Hildesheim the love of art displayed by Bishop Bernward, the tutor of Otto III, was also instrumental in producing sumptuously decorated books. According to the biography of his teacher Thangmar, the bishop was in the habit of studying artistic treasures on his travels, and establishing workshops at home where gifted young men had an opportunity of being educated. It even seems that the bishop himself was active in the art of manuscript illumination.

The Gospels, distinguished by Bernward's dedicatory inscription and probably executed during the second decade of the eleventh century, owe their effect not to the very great art of a highly trained draughtsman, but to the decoration which covers the entire page. Thangmar's assertion that Bernward was in the habit of copying what he considered most beautiful from all sorts of artistic works, is thus fully corroborated. Whereas motives like the groups of trees with the round symbols of the Evangelists (Plates 99 and 105) were taken over from the Franco-Saxon school, the tissue-like backgrounds and the blazing glories (Plates 100 and 102) are derived from the manuscripts of Echternach or Reichenau, and many figures remind us of these schools. The representation of the Maiestas Domini and the design of the Evangelists in the Ada group have also been utilized by Guntbald (Plate 103), while the high light in white in the ornaments reminds us of the school of St. Denis (the so-called school of Corbie). With these, however, intermingle reminiscences of some oriental models, as is shown in the miniatures of the Magi and in the horseshoe arches. The Crucifixion, too, in this and in the parallel codices, is represented with all different kinds of iconography. Nevertheless, the character is uniform, precisely because of the spinning over with ornament to which the schematic drawing of the figures is adapted. The ornamentation of the initials has more of the Franco-Saxon and Ratisbon than of the Reichenau manner (Plate 101).

The figures in the Bernward Bible (Plate 102) are likewise entirely woven into an ornamental net, and the form of the niches behind Moses and the Ecclesia is borrowed, as in Cologne (Plate 81b), from the corresponding setting behind St. Mary and St. John by the side of the cross, in eastern representations. This partiality for ornamentation is also inherited by later Hildesheim productions of the century, such as the so-called Gospels of Bishop Hezilo (Plate 105), the Evangelists of which show the influence of the Ada school. A small manuscript of the Gospels in the Berlin Kupferstichkabinett (Cod. 78 A. 1) shares all these characteristics.

The monastery of Fulda, geographically situated midway between Cologne and the Alamannic South, occupies also in the art of painting something like an intermediary position between the pictorial style of Cologne and the linear of Reichenau. In Fulda, which had already demonstrated its importance for literature and art during the ninth century, Carolingian models are reverted to as in other centres. A manuscript of the Gospels in the Municipal Library in Berlin (Vol. I, Plate 60) which, because it comes from Engern, is designated as the Codex Wittechindeus, is closely allied in its style to the Gospels in Erlangen coming from Fulda and executed in the ninth century. On the other hand, as far as the line drawing of some of the Evangelists and the ornamentation are concerned, it coincides exactly with the Fulda Sacramentary in Göttingen (Plate 106). The peculiarity of the vast group of manuscripts exhibiting the same style, and among which the Sacramentaries occupy the most prominent place, consists in the winding, weak lines, which are even more emphatically set by the application of a white tint on a combination of colour produced by blue-green and lilac tones. As for the ornamentation, the interlacings exhibit more of the band-like pattern and less of the tendril design, whereas in the richer plant material the artist frequently inclines towards a certain naturalism. Another peculi-

27

arity of these manuscripts is their preference for colonnades with an architrave which frame the scene either in several tiers one above the other or in
divisions placed in a row (Plate 108A). The result is an impression suggesting
mural paintings which, particularly in earlier times, exhibited such tiers
placed one above the other and divided by columns. Because most of these
manuscripts are Sacramentaries, scenes representing the Saints play a greater
rôle here than in any other scriptorium of the time (Plates 108 and 109). It
is particularly the martyrdom of St. Boniface, the founder and first abbot,
that is unavoidable. The calendar picture of a Berlin manuscript, interesting
on account of its contents (Plate 107), is, to judge from its style, undoubtedly a production of Fulda. Even now, although in a lesser degree than in
the time of Hrabanus, the activity of Fulda must have shone forth. Thus a
Sacramentary at Munich written for Corvey (Plate 111) exhibits the style of
Fulda, although it is still doubtful whether it was merely written for, or
executed in, Corvey. The uncoloured drawing contained in the same manuscript (Vol. I, plate 83B) points to further kindred productions in Westphalia
and Saxony, and the activity must presumably have extended down the
Weser as far as Bremen (Plate 98). A place by itself is occupied by a Sacramentary written in Fulda during the first half of the eleventh century and
preserved in Rome (Plate 110). In its more sharply drawn lines and in the
separation of the drapery motives it exhibits an influence received from the
South German Schools, and it thus more closely resembles the later productions of Ratisbon and Cologne. The careful and precise composition as
well as the architectural pattern lend to these two pictures, unfortunately the
only ones which remain in the manuscript, a monumental character. A Sacramentary in Lucca (Plate 112) approaches the works of the Fulda scriptorium in its manner of representing the scenes. The drawing, however, which
is sharper and more angular, shows a difference and approaches much more
the general style of the latter half of the eleventh century. The manuscript has
been assigned to Mainz.

A comparison of the sum of the manuscripts dating from the time of the

Saxon and first Salic Emperors with the productions of the Carolingian period now shows that the starting points in both cases were similar. Models
were also used in the last third of the tenth century, but they were the works
of the Carolingian period a century before, or contemporary Byzantine productions rather than early Christian, Italian or Syrian manuscripts. As in the
Carolingian period, the new craving for expression was responsible for a
transformation, but the tempo has grown quicker. The northern mediaeval
character becomes more evident as compared to classical tradition. The clever and adroit artists know how to utilize and adapt the strong influences
flowing from Byzantium, then in its second golden age. The artistic impulse
of imitation makes way for a creative gift and native skill. Thus, in spite
of many imitations, the specifically German style becomes more pronounced
than it had been in the Carolingian epoch, giving a purer representation of
the mediaeval spirit than is clearly witnessed at any time before the appearance of Gothic.

INDEX

31

32

37

PLATES 1-112

I

AIX-LA-CHAPELLE, CATHEDRAL TREASURY

GOSPELS OF OTTO II (973-83) OR III (983-1002)
(22 x 30 cm)

Dedicatory inscription:

HOC AVGVSTE LIBRO
TIBI COR DEVS INDVAT OTTO
QVEM DE LIVTHARIO
TE SVSCEPISSE MEMENTO

Reichenau, last quarter of the tenth century.

PAGE 31: GLORIFICATION OF OTTO. Above, the Emperor is crowned by the hand of God and surrounded by the symbols of the four Evangelists. Terra supports his throne. Two dukes pay him homage. Below are two warriors and two bishops.

Colours: In the miniatures of the Codex the following tints are employed: turquoise, dark blue, purple, azure, light coffee brown, sap green, Naples yellow, a little minium and various sorrel tones. The flesh tints are Naples yellow or brown.

BIBLIOGRAPHY

BEISSEL, *Otto-Hs.*
BOECKLER, p. 982 ff.
HASELOFF, *Egb. Psalter,* passim.
SCHRAMM, p. 80.
SWARZENSKI, I, p. 126.
VOEGE, p. 14, 43, ff. where note 2 gives a detailed account of earlier bibliography.

photo G. Mertens, Aix-la-Chapelle

2

AIX-LA-CHAPELLE, CATHEDRAL TREASURY

GOSPELS OF OTTO II OR III

SEE PLATE I

PAGE 52: THE THREE TEMPTATIONS OF CHRIST

COLOURS AND BIBLIOGRAPHY: *See plate I.*

photo G. Mertens, Aix-la-Chapelle

3

AIX-LA-CHAPELLE, CATHEDRAL TREASURY
GOSPELS OF OTTO II OR III

SEE PLATE I

PAGE 468: CHRIST AND THE THIEVES ON THE CROSS

COLOURS AND BIBLIOGRAPHY: *See plate* I.

photo G. Mertens, Aix-la-Chapelle

4

TRÈVES, STADTBIBLIOTHEK. Cod. 24 (21 x 27 cm)
Codex Egberti (Lectionary)

Executed about 980 at Reichenau by Kerald and Heribert for the archbi-shop Egbert of Trèves (977-993).

A. FOL. 78: WASHING OF THE FEET (cfr. plates 29 and 37)
By the painter who added the first pictures.

The sky is pink, the building is grey; the garments are white, the cloaks red, blue, violet and green (cf. Kraus).

B. FOL. 22: CHRIST AND THE CENTURIO (Matth. VIII, 5-13, cf. Luke, VII, 3-10).
Annotations (from left to right): AP(OSTO)LI PETRUS IHS XPC CENTURIO SENIORES IUD(EORUM). By the painter who added the first pictures.

The background is white and reddish. The drapery as in A., and also purple and orange. The faces are of an orange yellow tint with broad shades.

BIBLIOGRAPHY

BEISSEL, *Otto-Hs.*, p. 9 ff.
BOECKLER, p. 977 ff.
HASELOFF, *Egb. Psalter*, p. 59 ff. and passim.
FRANZ XAVER KRAUS, *Die Miniaturen des Codex Egberti in der Stadtbibl. zu Trier*, Freiburg, 1884 (reproduction).
SCHRAMM, p. 81 f.
WILH. VOEGE, *Ein Verwandter des Codex Egberti - Repert. f. Kstwiss.* XIX,
WILH. 1896, p. 105, 125. VOEGE, passim.

photo Baetz, Trèves

5

TRÈVES, STADTBIBLIOTHEK
Codex Egberti

See plate 4

Fol. 79ᵛ: Imprisonment (by the painter who continued the illuminations).

The sky is rose-coloured, the soil and the trees are greyish white, the drapery is in red, blue, violet, brown and white (cf. Kraus).

Bibliography: *see plate* 4.

photo Baetz, Trèves

Ihm naZarenum Dicat eis ihs Egosum

Stabat autem et iudas qui tradebat eum. cum
ipsis Ut ergo dixit eis egosum. abierunt retror
sum. et ceciderunt interram Iterum ergo interro
gauit eos Quem queritis? Illi autem dixerunt
Ihm naZarenum Respondit ihs. Dixi uobis. quia
egosum Si ergo me queritis. sinite hos abire

6

TRÈVES, STADTBIBLIOTHEK
CODEX EGBERTI

SEE PLATE 4

A. FOL. 8: CRUCIFIXION

Inscriptions: LATRONES · LONGINVS · TORTORES

The background is rose-coloured, the soil is green; for the rest, blue, white, ochre, red and gold are employed (cf. Kraus).

B. FOL. 17: ADORATION OF THE KINGS (by the painter who began the illuminations).

Marginal note: PVDIZAR (BALDAZAR?) MELCHIAS CASPAR

The flesh tint is pink laid on green. The drapery is dark red, green and blue and blue white. The architecture is violet with a red roof. The background is reddish. The colour technique is similar to that of the Ada group.

BIBLIOGRAPHY: *see plate* 4.

photo Baetz, Trèves

7

TRÈVES, STADTBIBLIOTHEK
REGISTRUM SCI. GREGORII

Fragment of 3 leaves, 19,8 x 27,1 cm. Trèves, c. 983, according to indication in the dedicatory verses which refer to the death of Otto II; it was executed for the Cathedral at Trèves at request of archbishop Egbert:

> Temporibus quondam tranquilla pace serenis
> Caesaris Ottonis Romana sceptra tenentis
> Italiae nec non Francorum jura regentis
> Hoc in honore tuo scriptum Petre sancte volumen
> Auro contectum gemmis pulcherrime comptum
> Ecbertus fieri jussit presul Trevirorum...
> Aurea quae perhibent, isto sub rege fuere
> Saecula...
> Sceptriger imperium qui postquam strenue rexit
> Decessit Romae tua ad atria, Petre Seculptus...
> (Printed entirely in BRAUN, e.c.)

FOL. 2: GREGORY WATCHED BY THE DEACON PETRUS

Inscription: Gregorius Papa. Notarius. *Bright ground in washed blue; for the
rest, the following tints predominate: suppressed bluish grey (Paenula of St Gregory, coat of the notary), unbroken blue relieved with white (alb), tawny (vessels)
toned down with white (dalmatic), tender pink working up to reddish violet (architecture and small curtain) light sea green (larger curtain). In addition to these
tints there are also green and sorrel tones in smaller spaces. The flesh is whitish
pink, shaded in green with bright sorrel drawing. The frame is purple with gold
ornamentation (cf. Haseloff).*

BIBLIOGRAPHY

BRAUN, p. 26, 35, 77 ff.
HASELOFF, *Egb. Psalter*, p. 60, 70 ff., 152 ff., ibid. also earlier bibliography.
SCHRAMM, p. 70 ff.

photo Staatl. Bildstelle, Berlin

8

CHANTILLY, MUSÉE CONDÉ
PICTURE GALLERY, NO 14 OF THE CAT. OF MSS.

SEE PLATE 7

SINGLE LEAF OF THE REGISTRUM GREGORII (belonging to plate 7). Otto II enthroned, surrounded by provinces paying homage.

Inscription: OTTO IMPERATOR AVGVSTVS.— GERMANIA FRANCIA ITALIA ALEMANIA

The background from bottom to top is green, greenish grey, light greyish blue and bright violet. The drapery of Otto is a bright violet. The cloak is minium red, the shoes golden. The canopy is green. All the nations have blue undergarments, yellowish brown, violet, sorrel and green upper garments; the headcloths are white shaded with green, yellowish brown or grey (cf. Haseloff).

BIBLIOGRAPHY

CHANTILLY, *Le Cabinet des Livres (Manuscrits)*, I, p. 16 f., Paris 1900.
HASELOFF, *Egb. Psalter*, p. 72 ff., ibid. further bibliography.
SCHRAMM, p. 70 ff.

photo Braun, Dornach-Paris

PARIS, BIBLIOTHÈQUE NATIONALE. Cod. lat. 8851
(28,5 x 38,5 cm)

GOSPELS FROM THE STE. CHAPELLE

to which it was presented 1379 by Charles V. Trèves. Probably by the master of the Registrum Gregorii (with the assistance of disciples). According to the annotations added to the medallions of the Emperors, fol. 16 (cf. plate 16A) it was executed between the coronation of Otto II (967) and his death (983).

FOL. 1: MAIESTAS DOMINI WITH THE EVANGELISTS AND THEIR SYMBOLS
(cf. plate 43).

Inscription of the Mandorla:

Η BACILEIA COY KYRIE BACILEIA ΠΑΝΤΩΝ
ΤΩΝ ΑΙΩΝΩ ΚΑΙ DICΠΟΤΕΙΑ COY
ΕΝ ΠΑCΕ ΓΕΝΕΑ ΚΑΙ ΓΕΝΕΑ

The annotations to the symbols of the Evangelists run as follows:

QUATTUOR HAEC DOMINUM SIGNANT ANIMALIA CHRISTUM
EST HOMO NASCENDO VITULUSQUE SACER MORIENDO
ET LEO SURGENDO CAELOS AQUILAQUE PETENDO
NEC MINUS HOS SCRIBAS ANIMALIA ET IPSA FIGURANT

The mandorla is in gold with white legend; the drapery of Christ is blue, the cloak red. The Evangelists are in green compartments. The inscriptions of the symbols are in gold (cf. Braun).

BIBLIOGRAPHY

BEISSEL, *Evang. Bch.,* p. 244.
BRAUN, p. 83 ff., ibid. detailed description and bibliography.
HASELOFF, *Egb. Psalter,* p. 75 ff. and passim.
SWARZENSKI I, p. 113, 115 note.
SWARZENSKI II, p. 28 notes 1 and 2.

photo Prof. Haseloff, Kiel

IO

PARIS, BIBLIOTHÈQUE NATIONALE. Cod. lat. 8851

See plate 9

Fol. 75ᵛ: The Evangelist Luke

The ground is green, blue in the lunette, the cloak is red with golden lights, the drapery is light blue (cf. Braun).

BIBLIOGRAPHY: *See plate* 9.

photo Prof. Haseloff, Kiel

II

PARIS, BIBLIOTHÈQUE NATIONALE. Cod. lat. 8851
See plate 9

Fol. 115ᵛ: The Evangelist John

The coat is blue, the cloak purple, the chair gold and green (cf. Braun).

BIBLIOGRAPHY: *See plate 9.*

photo Prof. Haseloff, Kiel

IOHANNES APOSTOLUS ET EUANGELISTA

12

CHANTILLY, MUSÉE CONDÉ
CABINET DES LIVRES, MS. 1447 (18 x 23,6 cm)

SACRAMENTARY

written for St. Nazarius of Lorsch. Trèves, probably by the master of the Registrum Gregorii, at the end of the tenth century, therefore probably the period of the Abbot Saleman of Lorsch (972-998). Fol. 147 at the bottom a Greek verse from the Psalms.

FOL. 4ᵛ: CRUCIFIXION WITH THE VIRGIN AND ST. JOHN

The inscriptions indicate only the names. The soil is olive, the background blue, towards the top violet. The drapery and the kerchief of the Virgin are bluish white, the paenula violet, dotted with gold. The tunic of St. John is violet, the loin-cloth of Christ is green with golden contours. The haloes are in gold. The flesh-tints are ochre with yellowish white lights and light blue contours. The hair of Christ and of St. John is dark grey.

BIBLIOGRAPHY

CHANTILLY, *Le Cabinet des Livres (Manuscrits)* I, p. 38 ff. (N. 40).
HASELOFF, *Egb. Psalter,* p. 77 ff., ibid. also further bibliography.
LEROQUAIS, I, p. 103 ff.

photo Prof. Haseloff, Kiel

13

A. MONASTERY AT STRAHOW NEAR PRAGUE
GOSPELS FROM ST. MARTIN NEAR TRÈVES
(SUPRA LITUS MOSELLAE)

Trèves, last quarter of the tenth century.

FOL. 106ᵛ: ST. LUKE (14 x 20 cm)

Legend: LUCAS AETHEREI SPECIEM TENET ORE JUVENCI

The background is in bright changing tints. The caption is golden on a dark violet ground. The drapery is bright blue, the cloak is moss green, the chair is golden with red cushion, the footstool is tawny, the desk dark violet. The frame is bright red (cf. Neuwirth).

BIBLIOGRAPHY
BEISSEL, *Evang. Bch.*, p. 244.
HASELOFF, *Egb. Psalter*, p. 148.
NEUWIRTH, in *Mittel. d. K. K. Zentr. Komm. z. Erh. und Erf. d. Kunst und hist. Denkmale.* N. F. XIV (1888), p. 88 ff.

B. BERLIN, STAATSBIBLIOTHEK. COD. THEOL. LAT. FOL. 283
(18 x 29 cm)
GOSPELS FROM ST. MAXIMIN, TRÈVES

Trèves, beginning of the eleventh century.

FOL. 88ᵛ: ST. LUKE

The background (in stripes) is white, greyish violet, greenish grey, bright brick red. The undergarment is lilac with white lights. The cloak is green, the footstool is grey with a whitish pink top. The symbol is dirty brown, the wings white with feathers drawn in lilac and a large black contour. The halo is in gold. Details uncoloured. The flesh is brownish with vigorous brown lines and shades touched up with white.

BIBLIOGRAPHY
HASELOFF, *Egb. Psalter*, p. 148.
BEISSEL, *Evang. Bch.*, p. 275.
SWARZENSKI II, p. 28 note 1.

14

A. COBLENZ, STAATSARCHIV. Cod. 701

GOSPELS FROM STA. MARIA AD MARTYRES AT TRÈVES

Trèves, last quarter of the tenth century.

FOL. 127: MAIESTAS DOMINI

BIBLIOGRAPHY

BEISSEL, *Evang. Bch.,* p. 275, ibid. further bibliographical references.
K. LAMPRECHT, *Initial-Ornamentik des VIII. bis XIII. Jhs.,* p. 21, No. 60,
plate 27. Leipzig 1882.

B. BERLIN, STAATSBIBLIOTHEK. Cod. THEOL. LAT. FOL. 283

SEE PLATE 13 B.

FOL. 11: CHRIST ENTHRONED ON THE GLOBE

surrounded by the seven candlesticks of the Apocalypse. In the terrestrial
globe at His feet is St. John.

*The background and the candlesticks are slate blue. Christ is in blue white drapery
and in pink cloak relieved with white. The edge of the cloth and the lining of the
alb are green. The big circle is tawny, whilst the small circle is bright and dark
grey. The cloak of St. John is terra de Siena colour. The collar and halo are dull
yellow. There is also a little gold. The flesh-tints are as in plate 13B, but the
iris and eyebrows are black.*

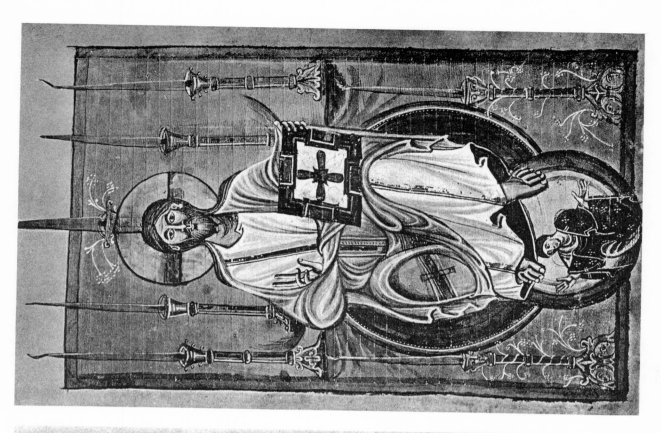

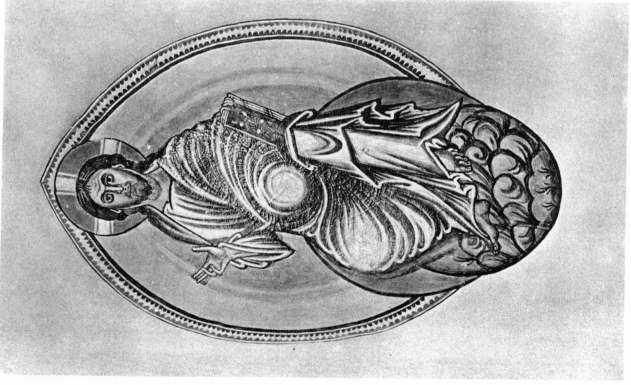

15

PARIS, BIBLIOTHÈQUE NATIONALE. Cod. 10501 (16 x 22,2 cm)

SACRAMENTARY

The Saints point to Trèves. In the twelfth century, arranged for the abbey of St. Symphorian in Metz. Trèves, last quarter of the tenth century.

A. FOL. 8ᵛ: BEGINNING OF CANON-TABLE. T(E IGITUR)

In the frame are the busts of the Beatitudines.

B. FOL. 9: CRUCIFIXION AND CONTINUATION OF THE CANON-TABLES

In the frame are the remaining four Beatitudines.

BIBLIOGRAPHY

HASELOFF, *Egb. Psalter,* p. 79, ibid. further bibliography.
LEROQUAIS I, p. 83 ff., pl. 16, ibid. further bibliography.
SWARZENSKI I, p. 114 note.
WEBER, p. 49 f., plates 103-107.

16

A. PARIS, BIBLIOTHÈQUE NATIONALE. Cod. lat. 8851

SEE PLATE 9

FOL. 16: TITLE PAGE TO ST. MATTHEW

with four Ottonian busts, probably of Henry I (twice), Otto I and II. Inscriptions of medallions: On top: OTTO IMPERATOR AVG ROMANOR. To the right: HENRICVS REX FRANCORV. Bottom: OTTO IVNIOR IMPE⁄ RATOR AVGVSTS. Left: HEINRICVS REX FRANCORVM.

The background is green with purple stripes. The frame has a gold bar and golden plait⁄work. The busts are drawn in white on a gold ground.

BIBLIOGRAPHY: *See plate 9.*

B. MANCHESTER, RYLANDS LIBRARY. Cod. 98 (19,3 x 20 cm)

GOSPELS

Cologne or Trèves, about 1000.

FOL. 16: ORNAMENTED PAGE

(Beginning of St. Matthew) with miniatures of the Ottonian Emperors on the margin (these miniatures seem to be those of Otto I, II and III). Inscription: top: ROMANE R. P. DIVE MEM. OTTO IMPER. AVG. right: XPIANE RELIGIONIS ET ROMANE R. P. OTTO IMP. bottom: A DO CORONATVS ROMANE R. P. OTTO IMPER. AVG. left: XPIANE RELIGIONES ET ROMANE R. P. OTTO IMP. AVG.

The ground is purple, green between the shoots with white rosettes in dots. The initials and tendrils are in gold. The plait⁄work is white. Chrysography. The outer border of the frame is red with a gold pattern, the inner part is gold with dark blue corners and variegated ornament. The medallions are gold in a blue frame.

BIBLIOGRAPHY

EHL, p. 197.
JAMES, p. 176 ff., plates 128⁄133.

17

DARMSTADT, LANDESBIBLIOTHEK. Cod. 1948
(22,2 x 29,8 cm)
SACRAMENTARY OF GERO

subsequently archbishop of Cologne (969/976). Reichenau, a short time prior to 969.

A. Fol. 6ᵛ: Gero presents the manuscript to St. Peter

The background to the right is in dull lilac, to the left in bright grey and green tints. The spandrels are in a green tint, the architecture is in blue, slate blue and lilac tones, and also in gold and silver. The drapery of St. Peter is lilac, the cloak slate blue, the cushion minium with silver. The alb of Gero is bright sea green, the paenula has two gradations of green with lining in minium. The haloes are golden. There are also details in gold and silver. The flesh-tints are pinkish grey with sea green shades, outlined in carmine red and black.

B. Fol. 5ᵛ: Maiestas Domini

The ground is blue and the tint in the spandrels is green. The frame of the medal-lions is in gold and silver with occasionally white on black. The drapery of Christ is blue with minium lining and brown clavi. The cloak is brownish violet, the cushion minium, the throne is entirely light dull lilac, green with gold and silver. The acanthus frame is in bright lilac, minium and blue tints with two gradations of green. The flesh-tints are greenish white with green shades, and black and red drawing (cf. plate 19).

BIBLIOGRAPHY

Boeckler, p. 958 ff.
Chroust, *Series I*, N. 19, plate 6.
Haseloff, *Egb. Psalter*, p. 119, 126 ff. and passim.
Koehler, *Adagruppe*, p. 255 ff.
Schmidt, reproduction.

18

A. KARLSBURG (GYULAFEHÉRVÁR), ROUMANIA
BATTHYÁNEUM
(26,8 x 36,7 cm)

GOSPELS OF ST. MATTHEW AND ST. MARK

From the Monastery of Lorsch (cf. I, plate 38 ff).

PAGE 26: THE EVANGELIST MATTHEW

BIBLIOGRAPHY

GOLDSCHMIDT I, p. 13.
HERMANN, p. 58.
KOEHLER, *Adagruppe*, p. 259 ff.
SCHMIDT, p. 51 ff.
R. SZENTIVÁNY, *Der Codex Aureus von Lorsch, jetzt in Gyulafehérvár-Stud.
und Mitt. z. Geschichte d. Benedikt. Ord. N. F. II* (1912), p. 131-151.

B. DARMSTADT, LANDESBIBLIOTHEK. COD. 1948
SEE PLATE 17

FOL. 1ᵛ: THE EVANGELIST MATTHEW

*The background is lilac, the arcade blue with golden ornaments and green bases, the
drapery is blue with white lights, lined in sorrel; the cloak is in minium with gold-
en inner drawing; the scroll is sorrel with a blue edge. The flesh-tints are pinkish
grey with brownish shades, red and black drawing.*

BIBLIOGRAPHY: *See plate 17.*

19

HEIDELBERG, UNIVERSITÄTSBIBLIOTHEK. Cod. Sal.IXb
(18,5 x 24 cm)
SACRAMENTARY FROM PETERSHAUSEN

Reichenau, ca. 980/990.

A. FOL. 40: THE ENTHRONED VIRGIN OR ECCLESIA

The dress is brownish lilac, the cloak slate blue with white lights and rosettes in a darker blue and gold. The seat is light sea green and bright pink. There are golden details. The hair is deep red. The flesh-tints are dull pink with green shades, with red and black inscriptions (cf. plate 17 B).

B. FOL. 41: MAIESTAS DOMINI

The ground is blue, the frame is in gold and silver on black. The drapery of Christ is blue with lining in minium, the cloak is in dull brownish violet. The throne is bright lilac and vellum-coloured, the cushion minium. The flesh tint and frame are as in A.

BIBLIOGRAPHY

BOECKLER, p. 966.
DE WALD, p. 87 ff.
HASELOFF, *Egb. Psalter*, p. 119 ff. and passim.
KOEHLER, *Adagruppe*, p. 259 ff.
OECHELHÄUSER, *Die Miniaturen der Univ. Bibl. Heidelberg*, 1887, p. 4 ff., pl. 1/2.

20

CIVIDALE, BIBLIOTECA. Cod. Gertrudianus (18,8 x 23,8 cm)

PSALTER

Written at Reichenau by Ruodprecht for archbishop Egbert of Trèves, (977-993).

FOL. 20ᵛ: KING DAVID

The background is bluish violet with golden animals. The cloak is dark purple merging into a brownish tint. The coat is bright blue with minium lining. The cushion is minium brown with a bright blue edge. The throne is glaucous, with some yellow and gold. The harp and crown are in gold. The drawing is generally brown and black. The flesh-tints are yellowish with bright green, seldom reddish shades, outlined in black, brown and red (cf. Haseloff).

BIBLIOGRAPHY

BOECKLER, p. 970 ff.
DEWALD, p. 87 ff.
HASELOFF, *Egb. Psalter* (reproduction).
KOEHLER, *Adagruppe,* note 1.
SCHRAMM, p. 81 f.

photo Prof. Haseloff, Kiel

21

CIVIDALE, BIBLIOTECA. Cod. Gertrudianus
See plate 20

A. Fol. 41ᵛ: St. Valerius

The alb is light blue, the dalmatic is shaded in light brown, green and grey, the chasuble has violet shades. The pallium is white, with minium lining in sleeves and hems. The halo is golden. The flesh-tints are as in plate 20. The frame consists of leaves drawn in gold and shaded in a vellum colour on purple.

B. Fol. 53: Initial B(eati) to Ps. xxxi

The letters, shoots and plait-knots are golden, drawn in minium. The gap in the letter and the background of plait-work knots is minium coloured. The background inside the initial is blue and green, outside purple with golden ornaments. The frame as in A (cf. Haseloff).

BIBLIOGRAPHY: *See plate 20.*

photo Prof. Haseloff, Kiel

22

PARIS, BIBLIOTHÈQUE NATIONALE. Ms. lat. 10514
(20,6 x 28,3 cm)

GOSPELS FROM THE ABBEY OF POUSSAY

Reichenau, last quarter of the tenth century, by the artist of the Egbert Psalter.

A. FOL. 30: THE ABBOT BETWEEN TWO ANGELS (left half of the dedication miniature).

B. FOL. 66ᵛ: THE ASCENSION OF CHRIST

The colours of the Codex resemble greatly those of the Egbert Psalter (plates 20-21); purple, light blue, minium and olive tints. The new tints are greyish (lilac and dark blue). Purple grounds (cf. Haseloff).

BIBLIOGRAPHY

BOECKLER, p. 974 ff.
DE WALD, p. 87 ff.
HASELOFF, *Egb. Psalter,* p. 81 ff. and passim.
KOEHLER, *Adagruppe,* p. 271.
SCHRAMM, p. 82.

photo Prof. Haseloff, Kiel

23

SOLOTHURN, SACRISTY OF THE COLLEGIATSTIFT

SACRAMENTARY

Written for Abbot Adalbert of Hornbach by Eburnant. Latter half of the tenth century. Reichenau, last quarter of the tenth century.

PRESENTATION OF THE BOOK TO CHRIST BY ST. PETER

BIBLIOGRAPHY

BOECKLER, p. 969.
HASELOFF, *Egb. Psalter,* p. 83, 115, 123 ff.
SWARZENSKI, II, p. 6, 16 note 6.

photo Prof. Haseloff, Kiel

24

MUNICH, STAATSBIBLIOTHEK. Cod. lat. 4453 (cim. 58)
(24,5 x 34,7 cm)
GOSPELS FROM THE CATHEDRAL TREASURY AT BAMBERG

Reichenau, end of the tenth century.

A. FOL. 23ᵛ: THE PROVINCES PAYING HOMAGE TO THE EMPEROR (from right to left: Slavinia, Germania, Gallia and Roma).

The background from bottom to top is light green, light slate blue, and pinkish lilac. The undergarments of Slavinia and Gallia are bluish white, of Germania and Roma are a neutral blue tint. The cloaks are violet, light green, pinkish lilac merging into ruby and orange yellow. The cloth under the bowl is minium. The flesh-tints of Slavinia and Gallia are brownish pink, of the two others pale yellow with greenish grey shades. There is gold in the crowns, borders and vessels.

B. FOL. 24: THE ENTHRONED EMPEROR (probably Otto III) and his suite.

The background is similar to that of A. Otto is in a white-blue undergarment, violet dalmatic, and light green cloak. The curtain is olive green and pink lilac working up to a ruby tint. The throne canopy is minium, the cushion is in a neutral brown tint. The remaining figures are bluish white, dark bluish violet, dark blue and minium. The roof is minium, the details are golden. The flesh-tints change as in A.

BIBLIOGRAPHY

BOECKLER, p. 989 ff.
CHROUST, *Series I,* No. 19, plates 9 and 10.
HASELOFF, *Egb. Psalter,* p. 72 ff. and passim.
LEIDINGER, I (reproduction); ibid. further bibliography.
LEIDINGER, *Meisterwerke,* Plates 5 and 6.
SCHRAMM, p. 59 ff., 69 f.
VOEGE, p. 7 ff. and passim.

25

MUNICH, STAATSBIBLIOTHEK. Cod. lat. 4453

See plate 24

Fol. 25ᵛ: The Evangelist Matthew

Legend: P[ER] CONFORME SVI MATHEV[M] CERNE NOTARI. In the haloes above ESAY[AS] and OSEAS, below ABRAH[AM]

The background inside the columns and arcades is golden, outside dark violet. The circle in the middle is light green, the haloes above and below are light violet. The edge and wings of angels are partly lilac and partly dark brown. The haloes round the four prophets and Abraham are in light green. St. Matthew, dark lilac (upper garment), light blue (undergarment), both relieved with white. The flesh-tints are yellowish red, relieved with white. The hair is always blue, only that of the angels is black. The inscription line at the bottom is gold, otherwise white. The tympanum of the arcade is set in a light green frame. The ornament is in gold, blue and lilac, the capitals of the columns are reddish violet, the shaft of the columns is moss green and black.

BIBLIOGRAPHY: *See plate 24.*

photo Reusch, Munich

26

Fol. 139ᵛ: The Evangelist Luke

Inscription: FONTE PATRVM DVCTAS BOS AGNIS ELICIT VNDAS
In the haloes: ABACVC EZE[CHIEL] D[AVI]D NA[VM] SOPHON[IAS]

Very uniform in colour scheme. The haloes are bluish grey, white grey and dull green, the drinking animals are light grey and sea green. The symbol is yellowish merging into grey. The flesh-tint is brownish pink. The ground in the arcade and the large medallion is golden, outside it is purple; the cloak of St. Luke and the shafts of the columns are purple brown. The undergarment is bluish white, the mandorla is dull green.

BIBLIOGRAPHY: *See plate 24.*

photo Reusch, Munich

27

MUNICH, STAATSBIBLIOTHEK. Cod. lat. 4453
See plate 24

FOL. 32ᵛ: THE BAPTISM AND THE THREE TEMPTATIONS OF CHRIST

The background is in gold. The flesh-tints of the figures are light brown, relieved with a reddish tint. Upper representation: the draperies are in minium, light blue, light brown and dark violet. The main space is tawny. Lower representation: the architecture to the left is light blue and tawny; the robes are violet and red. The draperies and haloes as above (the haloes in dark blue and green tints). The Devil has black hair and light brown wings. His drapery is greyish violet.

BIBLIOGRAPHY: *See plate 24.*

photo Reusch, Munich

28

MUNICH, STAATSBIBLIOTHEK. Cod. lat. 4453

See plate 24

Fol. 167ᵛ: The parable of the Good Samaritan (Luke X, 30-35)

The outer frame is dark violet with lighter ornament outlined with white. The background of the representation is gold, with a frame outlined with light green, white and red tints. The architecture is as in Pl. 27. The mount on top and in the middle is light brown, beneath it is bluish grey. The colours of the drapery are light green, light and dark blue, minium and light brown. The stockings are always light blue. The contours of the figures are mostly white.

BIBLIOGRAPHY: *See plate 24.*

photo Reusch, Munich

29

MUNICH, STAATSBIBLIOTHEK. COD. LAT. 4453

SEE PLATE 24

FOL. 237: THE WASHING OF THE FEET

The frame is dark brownish violet, the background from top to bottom is light blue gradually changing to a reddish violet tint. The architecture is as in Pl. 27. The bases of the columns and the shafts are light green with black and white dots. The space enclosed by the columns and architecture is golden. The flesh-tints are ochro-leous with light brown shades. The drapery is light blue, light grey and pea green. The soil is dirty dark brown.

BIBLIOGRAPHY: *See plate 24.*

photo Reusch, Munich

30

BAMBERG, STAATSBIBLIOTHEK. Cod. bibl. 76 (A. I. 43)
(19 x 25 cm)

COMMENTARY ON ISAIAH

from the Bamberg Cathedral library. Reichenau, end of the tenth century.

FOL. 10: VISION OF ISAIAH

Purple leaf, the spandrels in a lighter, more brownish purple with gold drawing. The oblong middle compartment is turquoise coloured. The inner part of halo is golden. Otherwise, only the following tints are employed: light blue, violet, green and light brown merging into violet.

BIBLIOGRAPHY

FISCHER, I (reproduction).
HASELOFF, *Egb. Psalter,* p. 57.

31

BAMBERG, STAATSBIBLIOTHEK. Cod. bibl. 22 (A. I. 47)
(19 x 25 cm)

COMMENTARY ON DANIEL

from the Bamberg Cathedral library. Reichenau, end of the tenth century.

FOL. 32: INITIAL A(NNO) WITH THE WRITING DANIEL

The ground inside the arcade is uncoloured, outside it is purple with a green edge; in the spandrels there is bright purple with white and blue ornaments. The figures are purple, light blue and light brown. The haloes are golden. The flesh-tints are light brownish, retouched with white and drawn in black. The hair is grey. The initial is drawn in a red gold tint on a blue and green ground. Chrysography.

BIBLIOGRAPHY

FISCHER (reproduction).
VOEGE, p. 99 f.

32

ROME, VATICANA, Barb. lat. 711 (formerly xiv, 84)
(21 x 23 cm)

Evangelistary

Reichenau, about 1000.

Fol. 11: The Evangelist John

BIBLIOGRAPHY

Haseloff, *Egb. Psalter*, p. 93, 102, 106, 157 f.
Swarzenski I, p. 108 note, 117 note.
Voege, p. 93, 151.

photo Staatl. Bildstelle, Berlin

33

ROME, VATICANA. Barb. lat. 711
See plate 32

Fol. 8: The nativity of Christ with the shepherds adoring and the Annunciation to the shepherds.

Bibliography: *See plate 32.*

photo Staatl. Bildstelle, Berlin

salnum facie populum suum a peccatis eor ii

34

MUNICH, STAATSBIBLIOTHEK. Cod. lat. 23338
(17,7 x 23,5 cm)

EVANGELISTARY

Reichenau, first quarter of eleventh century.

FOL. 158ᵛ: PARABLE OF THE DEBTOR (MATTH. XVIII, 23-35)

Above he is kneeling before his master, to the right he is strangling his
own debtor, below he is being thrown into prison.

*The representation on the top is on gold ground, dirty green soil. The architecture
is bluish white. The tints in the drapery are dark purple, minium and a lighter
and darker bluish grey. In the lower picture the colours in the drapery are as on
the top; the background and soil are white, the architecture is brown and red
(brick roof).*

BIBLIOGRAPHY

BEISSEL, *Bernward-Evang.*, p. 40.
HASELOFF, *Egb. Psalter*, p. 90.
SWARZENSKI I, p. 118, 144.
VOEGE, p. 142 f.

photo Reusch, Munich

35

MUNICH, STAATSBIBLIOTHEK. Cod. lat. 4452 (cim. 57)
(32 x 42,5 cm)

Gospels from the Cathedral treasury at Bamberg

Written in Reichenau between 1002 and 1014 for Henry II, who presented it to his foundation Bamberg, cf. the dedicatory verses fol. 1ᵛ:

REX HEINRICVS...
OBTVLIT HVNC LIBRVM..
.... IN DONARIA TEMPLI
....
O PETRE CVM PAVLO GENTIS DOCTORE BENIGNO ....
HVNC TIBI DEVOTVM PRECE FAC SVPER ASTRA BEATVM
CVM CVNIGVNDA SIBI CONREGNANTE SERENA.............

A. FOL. 3ᵛ: THE EVANGELIST MATTHEW

Inscription: REX NOTAT HIC HOMINIS. MATTHEVS SCRIPTOR HERILIS

The ground between the columns is golden, in the lunette it is lilac, outside it is purple. The architrave is purple. The undergarments are light blue, the cloak of St. Matthew is violet, of the angel olivaceous. The wings of the angel are lilac grey, the curtains are green and carmine, the shafts of the columns light blue. In addition to these tints there are also employed brick red, dark grey and blue, light brown, orange colour and gold (cf. Leidinger).

B. FOL. 4: THE EVANGELIST MARK

Inscription: UT LEO VOCE FREMIT. MARCVS DVM TALIA SCRIBIT

The background is as in A. in the lunette the tint changes from lilac grey to pink. The drapery and lower side of the wings are light blue, the cloak blackish blue with green lights. The symbol is brown, the shafts of the big columns are brick red. For the rest, the colours employed are: light blue, brick red, brown, carmine, dull tawny, green and gold.

BIBLIOGRAPHY

Boeckler, p. 992 ff.
Chroust, *Series I*, N. 20, pl. 2⁄4.
Haseloff, *Egb. Psalter*, passim.
Leidinger V (reproduction), ibid. earlier bibliography.
Leidinger, *Meisterwerke*, pl. 8⁄11. ⁄ Schramm, p. 56 ff.
Voege, p. 112 and passim. ⁄ Woelfflin, p. 14 ff.

photo Reusch, Munich

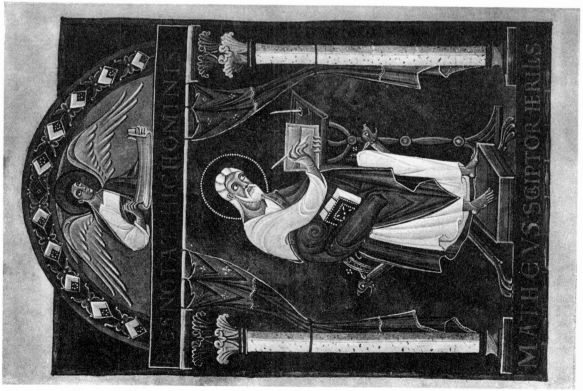

36

MUNICH, STAATSBIBLIOTHEK. Cod. lat. 4452

See plate 35

FOL. 8ᵛ: ANNUNCIATION TO THE SHEPHERDS

The background is golden, the upper stripe is brownish pink, the cloaks are brownish green. The undergarments of the two large figures are light blue, the cloak of the angel is orange coloured, that of the shepherd is minium. The wings are light slate blue. The drapery of the two seated figures is deep sea green and brownish grey. The colour of the sheep is either light blue or orange. The flesh-tints of the angel are brownish pink with sorrel shades. There is a little black in the drawing and white lights. The flesh-tints of the shepherd are vigorous sorrel.

BIBLIOGRAPHY: *See plate 35.*

photo Reusch, Munich

37

Fol. 105ᵛ: Last Supper and Washing of the feet (cf. pl. 4A and 29)

Golden ground. There is much light blue in the undergarments of Christ and of almost all the disciples and in the table cloth (green shades here). A brown lilac tint is employed in the cloaks of Christ, of Judas and those of several seated disciples. A yellow tint is used in the cloaks of St. Peter, in the coat of Judas and of the cup-bearer to the left. In smaller spaces the following colours are used: dark grey, slate blue, dark blue, light and dark green, tawny, carmine, sorrel, and brown (cf. Leidinger).

BIBLIOGRAPHY: *See plate 35.*

photo Reusch, Munich

38

A. MUNICH, STAATSBIBLIOTHEK. Cod. lat. 4452

SEE PLATE 35

FOL. 12: INITIALS IN (PRINCIPIO ERAT)

The initials are golden, the drawing, interior background of the letter and plait-work knots vermilion. The ground behind the letter N is blue and green; for the rest, there is a vellum ground with purple stripes. Chrysography.

BIBLIOGRAPHY: *See plate 35.*

B. MUNICH, STAATSBIBLIOTHEK. Cod. lat. 4454 (CIM. 59)
(23,3 x 30,5 cm)

GOSPELS FROM BAMBERG

Reichenau, beginning of the eleventh century.

FOL. 195: INITIALS IN (PRINCIPIO ERAT)

The initials and grounds inside the acanthus frame are as in A., outside they are purple. The frame edge is red with gold ornaments. The acanthus is pink, the corner blossoms are dark red and light green (cf. Leidinger).

BIBLIOGRAPHY: *See plate 40.*

39

BAMBERG, STAATSBIBLIOTHEK. Cod. bibl. 140 (A. II. 42)
(20,4 x 29,5 cm)

Apocalypse and Evangelistary from St. Stephen's in Bamberg. Written for
Henry II at Reichenau (the Ms. had a gold cover on which were named
Henry II and Cunigund). Reichenau, first quarter of eleventh century (prior
to 1020).

Fol. 49ᵛ: The beast and the false prophet thrown into hell, the
others are slain with the sword (Revelations XIX, 20/21).

BIBLIOGRAPHY

Schramm, p. 56 ff.
Voege, p. 139 ff.
Woelfflin, reproduction. Ibid. p. 38 note 1/10, further bibliography.

40

MUNICH, STAATSBIBLIOTHEK. Cod. lat. 4454 (cim. 59)
(23,3 x 30,5 cm)
GOSPELS

From the Cathedral treasury of Bamberg (cf. plate 38B). Reichenau, begin‚
ning of the eleventh century.

A. Fol. 86ᵛ: The Evangelist Mark with the rising Christ

Inscription:

ECCE LEO FORTIS TRANSIT DISCRIMINA MORTIS
FORTIA FACTA STVPET MARCVS QVI NVNTIA DEFERT

The ground inside is golden, outside purple, in the lunette it changes from lilac to pinkish white. The architrave is purple. The coat of St. Mark is light blue, the cloak dark blue and green. The shafts of the columns have two gradations of a green tint. Besides these colours there are also the usual sorrel, light blue, slate blue, green and gold.

B. Fol. 194ᵛ: The Evangelist John with the Ascension of Christ

Inscription:

MAXIMVS ECCE GIGANS SCANDIT SVPER ASTRA TRIVMPHANS
COMPROBAT ISTA VIDENS SVBLATVS IN ORA JOHANNES

The background and the architrave are as in A. The colour of the undergarment of St. John is light blue, the cloak lilac, the chair is brown with green canopy, the shafts of the columns are sea green with red and a little white. In the smaller spaces the following colours are used: Light blue, tawny, carmine, brick red, green, brown, lilac, dull yellow and gold (cf. Leidinger).

BIBLIOGRAPHY

CHROUST, *Series I*, No 20, pl. 7 and 8.
HASELOFF, *Egb. Psalter*, p. 88, 106, 110 ff., 154.
LEIDINGER VI, reproduction, ibid. further bibliography.
LEIDINGER, *Meisterwerke*, pl. 7.
SCHRAMM, p. 61 note, 62 note.
VOEGE, p. 129 ff.

41

COLOGNE, CATHEDRAL LIBRARY. Cod. 218
(20,6 x 28,5 cm)
Gospels

From the monastery of Limburg on the Hardt, where, according to an entry made in the twelfth century, it was provided with a costly binding. Reichenau, first quarter of eleventh century.

Fol. 163^v: The Apostle John

BIBLIOGRAPHY

Haseloff, *Egb. Psalter,* p. 106.
Merton, p. 85.
Voege, p. 145 f.

photo Staatl. Bildstelle, Berlin

42

COLOGNE, CATHEDRAL LIBRARY. Cod. 218

See plate 41

Fol. 109: Q(uoniam quidem)

Bibliography: *See plate* 41.

43

GOTHA, LANDESBIBLIOTHEK. I, 19. Codex aureus
(30,5 x 44 cm)
Gospels of Otto III

Executed at Echternach between 983 (accession to the throne of Otto III) and 991 (death of Theophano). On the cover are Otto III and Theophano and the patrons of Echternach.

Page 5: Maiestas Domini. With the symbols of the Evangelists and the four major prophets (cf. plate 9). In the mandorla there is an illegible legend in Greek letters.

Purple leaf. The large frame is in white body-colour. The middle field is bright blue. The mandorla and the medallions with the symbols are golden. The backgrounds with the Evangelists are yellowish green. The inscriptions are white. The tunic of Christ is white and blue, the cloak is light blue with yellowish green shades. The borders, clavi and the lining of the alb are in minium. The drapery of the remaining figures exhibits partly the same colours and partly bright and dark lilac, violet brown, yellowish brown and dark green, all the colours in darkly shaded gradations. The same colours are also used in the symbols, where greenish grey, yellow, and brownish pink are employed. The flesh-colour is a reddish brown with darker (Christ) or reddish shades; the drawing is brown and partly black.

BIBLIOGRAPHY

Beissel, *Otto Hs.,* p. 18 ff.
Beissel, *Upsala,* 6, 22.
Braun, p. 94 ff.
Chroust, *Series II,* N. 9, pl. 7-10.
Haseloff, *Egb. Psalter,* p. 147, 150, 151 and passim.
Jahrbücher des Vereins d. Altertumsfreunde im Rheinland, 70, p. 78 ff.
Michel, I, 2, p. 726 f.
Schramm, p. 65.
Swarzenski, I, p. 53, 110 note, 113 f., 115 note, 144 note.
Swarzenski, II, passim.
Voege, p. 380 f., ibid. earlier bibliography.

photo Prof. Haseloff, Kiel

44

GOTHA, LANDESBIBLIOTHEK. COD. I, 19

SEE PLATE 43

A. PAGE 40: ST. MATTHEW

Inscription: CARNE D[EV]M VOCE MATHEVS SIGNAT ET ORE.

Purple leaf. White frame. The ground from bottom to top is light blue, greyish blue, pale lilac, and golden in the lunette. The drapery is white and blue, the cloak is yellow and brown, the chair-hangings are minium, the cushions and curtains are green with golden flowers and borders. The angel has a white and blue garment and a minium coloured cloak. The wings are in pink lilac and brownish green. The stripes with the legend are in purple and gold. In the remaining portions of the plate lilac, green, light blue, minium, purple and gold are employed. The flesh-colour is grey, partly of a greenish hue, with brownish violet shades, drawn in violet brown and black.

B. PAGE 108: ST. MARK AS BISHOP

Inscription: FORTIOR EST OMNI QVEM SIGNAS MARCE LEONE

The light frame is thinly laid on. The background is in light blue with green in the lunette. The masonry is lilac. The alb is white with light blue, the dalmatic bright yellow, and the chasuble purple. The cushions and the book edge are minium. The symbol is greyish yellow, the wings are bright blue with a yellowish green and lilac. The shafts of the big external columns are purple with minium and white, those of the inner columns are green and white, golden and black. The flesh-colour is like that exhibited in plate 43.

BIBLIOGRAPHY: *See plate 43.*

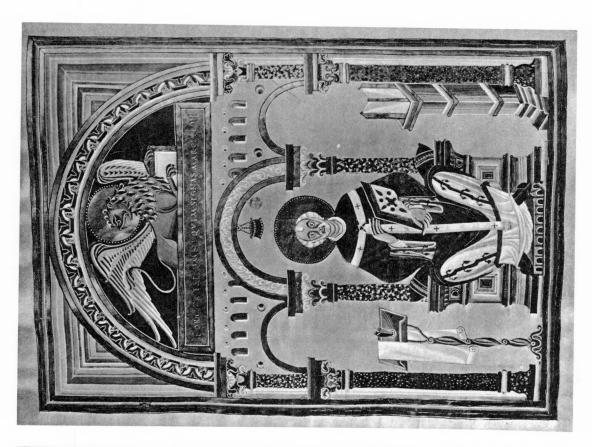

45

GOTHA, LANDESBIBLIOTHEK. Cod. I, 19

See plate 43

Page 224: The Evangelist John

The frame is as in plate 44B. The ground is golden and light blue in the lunette. The stripes inside the acanthus-frame are light blue. The alb is whitish blue, the cloak purple. The chair-hangings are green; the scaffolding of the throne is light blue with gold and white; the cushions are minium. The stripes with the legends are in purple and gold. The shafts of the big columns are in dark green, marbled with white, minium and black. The body of the eagle is a greyish green, the head is a light slate-colour, and the wings are lilac, light blue and ochre. In the remaining portions of the plate the same colours are used as in the preceding plates. The flesh-colour is a brownish yellow with violet brown shades and a violet brown and black drawing.

Bibliography: *See plate 43.*

46

GOTHA, LANDESBIBLIOTHEK. Cod. I, 19

See plate 43

Page 36: Annunciation, Visitation, Nativity. Adoration of the Shepherds. The visit of the Kings to Herod.

Purple leaf. The frame is in a white body-colour. The backgrounds are green, light blue, light greenish blue and lilac, always separated one from the other by architectures. In the remaining portions of the plate lilac, pink lilac, light greenish grey, green and golden colours are exhibited in variegated alternation. The frame stripes are golden with green inscriptions. The flesh-colour is yellowish with orange-coloured but also with greenish shades. The features are in minium and black colours.

Bibliography: *See plate 43.*

47

GOTHA, LANDESBIBLIOTHEK. Cod. I, 19

See plate 43

Canon Table

Colours:

The legend stripes are purple and gold. The inner lunette is light blue, the outer green. The shafts of the columns are light blue, minium, marbled in slate blue and gold; the winding column is green. The details are in blue, green, lilac, minium and golden colours.

BIBLIOGRAPHY: *See plate 43.*

48

GOTHA, LANDESBIBLIOTHEK. COD. I, 19

SEE PLATE 43

FOL. 51^v: ORNAMENTED PAGE WITH TEXTILE PATTERNS

The stripes from bottom to top are: Green with white and yellowish brown. Minium with dark green and white. Light greyish blue of a green hue with lilac, yellow brown, minium and green. Pale lilac with green and minium. Pink lilac with green and minium. Green with bistre and minium. Minium with dark green and white. Light greyish blue of a green hue, with yellowish green and dark green. In the remaining portions of the plate the same patterns and colours are used. The external frames are purple with light greyish blue dots; the inner frame is in minium.

BIBLIOGRAPHY: *See plate 43.*

49

A. GOTHA, LANDESBIBLIOTHEK. Cod. I, 19

SEE PLATE 43

INITIAL PAGE B(EATO PAPAE DAMASO). *Purple leaf.*

The frame is in white body-colour. The background is in a vigorous green with white and minium red small flowers. The inside of the initial is lilac with light blue and white dots and lines. The letters and tendrils are in gold, drawn in red. The plait-work, the mask and the letter spaces are lilac and white. The acanthus work is blue, minium, green and lilac, between golden stripes.

BIBLIOGRAPHY: *See plate 43.*

B. MADRID, ESCORIAL. Codex Aureus (23 x 37 cm)

EVANGELIARY FROM SPEYER

Contains dedicatory miniatures of the Emperor Conrad II and of his wife Gisela, as well as that of King Henry III with Agnes. Echternach. Between 1043 (Marriage with Agnes) and 1046 (Coronation of Henry as Emperor).

INITIAL PAGE B(EATO PAPAE DAMASO)

BIBLIOGRAPHY: *See plate 57.*

photo Moreno, Madrid

50

PARIS, BIBLIOTHÈQUE NATIONALE. Nouv. acquis. 2196

GOSPELS FROM LUXEUIL (FRAGMENT)

Written for Abbot Gérard of Luxeuil. Echternach, beginning of the eleventh century.

THE EVANGELIST MARK

Inscription: MARCE TVIS SCRIPTIS VOX EST SIMILATA LEONIS

BIBLIOGRAPHY

BRAUN, p. 83.
BEISSEL, *Upsala*, 6.
BEISSEL, *Evang. Bch.*, p. 246.
HASELOFF, *Egb. Psalter*, p. 92, 151.
MICHEL, I, 2, p. 727.
SWARZENSKI, I, p. 110 note, 113, 115 note, 147 note.

photo Prof. Haseloff, Kiel

MARCE TVIS SCRIPTIS VOX EST SIMILATA LEONIS

51

PARIS, BIBLIOTHÈQUE NATIONALE. Cod. lat. 10438
(18,5 x 26,5 cm)

EVANGELIARY

According to an entry of the eighteenth century it was presented by Bishop Adalbero II of Metz (984⁄1005) to the Collegiate Church of St. Salvator at Metz. Echternach, beginning of the eleventh century.

A. FOL. 24: ANNUNCIATION   B. FOL. 65: BIRTH OF CHRIST

BIBLIOGRAPHY

HASELOFF, *Egb. Psalter*, p. 83, 90, 101.
SWARZENSKI, I, p. 115 note.
SWARZENSKI, II, p. 28 notes 1 and 2, 32 note 3.
VOEGE, p. 380, ibid. earlier bibliography.
WEBER, p. 45 ff., pl. 89⁄100.

photo Prof. Haseloff, Kiel

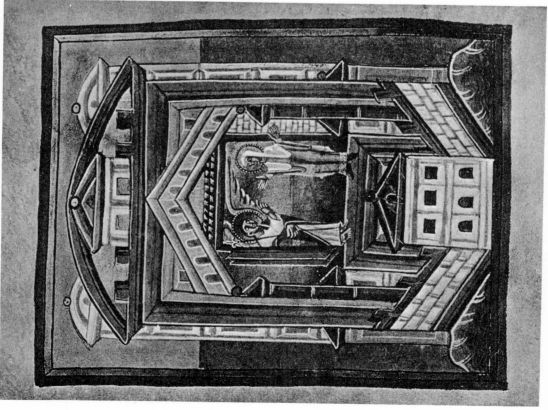

52

BREMEN, STADTBIBLIOTHEK
BOOK OF PERICOPES OF HENRY III (14,5 x 18,5 cm)

Written at Echternach between 1039 (accession to throne of Henry III) and
1040 (marriage with Agnes). Cf. plate 53.

A. FOL. 124^V: TWO SCRIBES OF ECHTERNACH

The work has been done by two scribes of Echternach (a monk and a
layman).

Inscription: O REX ISTE TVVS LOCVS EPTERNACA VOCATVS

                  EXPECTAT VENIAM NOCTE DIEQVE TVAM

The monk is in a brown cowl, the layman in a red coat.

B. FOL. 125: PRESENTATION OF THE MANUSCRIPT TO THE KING

Inscription: HIC REX HEINRICVS NVLLI PROBITATE SECVNDVS

                  REGNVM IVSTITIA REGIT ET PIETATE PATERNA

On the book: SALVS NOSTRA IN MANV TVA

                 RESPICIAT SUPER NOS MISERICORDIA TVA

BIBLIOGRAPHY

BEISSEL, *Otto Hs.,* p. 28. ff., 63 ff.
BEISSEL, *Upsala,* 6, 16, 18, 41.
BEISSEL, *Evang. Bch.,* p. 214 f., 222, 245, 345.
BRAUN, p. 94 and passim.
CHROUST, *Series II,* N. 10, pl. 1 and 2.
HASELOFF, *Egb. Psalter,* passim.
Mitteilg. d. K. K. Centr. Komm. z. Erb. u. Erf. d. Kunst u. hist. Denkm. VII
    (1862), p. 57 ff.
SWARZENSKI, I, p. 72 note, 73, 91 note, 113 f.
SWARZENSKI, II, p. 35 note 3.
VOEGE, p. 383.

photo Prof. Haseloff, Kiel

53

BREMEN, STADTBIBLIOTHEK
LECTIONARY OF HENRY III
SEE PLATE 52

A. FOL. 3: REPRESENTATION OF THE EMPRESS GISELA

Inscription:

> PAX ERIT IN MVNDO DVM GISELA VIXERIT ISTO
> QVAE GENVIT REGEM POPVLOS PIETATE REGENTEM

The background is green, Gisela wears a purple brown undergarment and a light blue paenula.

B. FOL. 3ᵛ: REPRESENTATION OF HENRY

Inscription:

> HEINRICUM REGEM JUVENILE FLORE NITENTEM
> AD LAVDEM REGNI CONSERVET GRATIA CHRISTI

The background is blue. The Emperor is arrayed in a golden cloak, blue coat and purple brown stockings.

BIBLIOGRAPHY: *See plate 52.*

photo Prof. Haseloff, Kiel

54

BREMEN, STADTBIBLIOTHEK
LECTIONARY OF HENRY III

SEE PLATE 52

A. FOL. 23ᵛ: THE HEALING OF THE BLIND AT JERICHO (Luke XVIII, 31-43).
The ground below is green, towards the top it is reddish.

B. FOL. 66: THE DOUBTING THOMAS (John XX, 26-29).
Inscription: VT D(OMI)N(V)M CREDAS HOMINE TV DIDYDME(M) PALPAS

BIBLIOGRAPHY: *See plate 52.*

photo Prof. Haseloff, Kiel

55

BREMEN, STADTBIBLIOTHEK

LECTIONARY OF HENRY III

SEE PLATE 52

FOL. 78ᵛ/79: THE PARABLE OF THE SUPPER (Luke XVI, 16/24).
Inscription:

AD CENAM MAGNAM VOCAT HIC MVLTOS HOMO QVIDAM
CAECOS ET CLAUDOS NEC NON INVITAT EGENOS
EXCVSAS CVR TE DECEPTE CVPIDINE VILLAE
SVNT MICHI QVINQVE BOVM IVGA QVAE NVNC VADO PROBATVM
VXOREM DVXI RESPONDIT TERTIVS ISTI

BIBLIOGRAPHY: *See plate 52.*

photo Rheinisches Museum, Cologne

56

BRUSSELS, BIBLIOTHÈQUE ROYALE. Cod. 9428
(14 x 20,5 cm)
LECTIONARY

Executed for a church of St. Stephen and in the twelfth century already in the possession of the Cathedral at Bremen. Echternach, second quarter of the eleventh century.

A. FOL. 23: HEALING OF THE LEPER

B. THE FINDING OF THE FOUR COFFINS WITH THE RELICS OF THE SAINTS STEPHANUS, NICODEMUS, GAMALIEL AND HIS SON ABIBAS

Inscription:

ALTER ADEST TESTIS MONSTRANS LOCA PLENA BEATIS.

MIGETIVS. LVCIANVS.

BIBLIOGRAPHY

BEISSEL, *Bernward-Evang.*, p. 30 ff.
BEISSEL, *Upsala*, p. 16, 41.
BEISSEL, *Evang. Bch.*, p. 215, 222, 246, 248, 344.
BRAUN, p. 97.
HASELOFF, *Egb. Psalter*, p. 88, 95, 101, 103.
SWARZENSKI, I, p. 91 note, 110 note, 113, 115 note.
SWARZENSKI, II, p. 32 note 3, 33 note 4, 35 note 3.
VOEGE, p. 384, ibid. also earlier bibliography.

57

MADRID, ESCORIAL. Codex Aureus (35 x 50 cm)
Gospels from Speyer

Written at Echternach for Henry III between 1043 (marriage with Agnes) and 1046 (Coronation as Emperor).

FOL. 2ᵛ: ENTHRONED CHRIST WITH THE IMPERIAL PAIR CONRAD («Cu-onradus Imp.») AND GISELA («Gisela Imperat»). In the frame the symbols of the four Evangelists. In the Mandorla there is an inscription in Greek letters:

BHNHΔIKΘVC NΩMHN MAIHCΘAΘIC IN AHΘHPNV̄ HΘ PHΠΛHBIΘVP
MAIHCΘ(AΘH H)IVC OMNIC ΘHPPA.

In the frame:

ANTE TVVM VVLTVM MEA DEFLEO CRIMINA MVLTVM
DA VENIAM MEREAR CVIVS SVM MVNERE CAESAR
PECTORE CVM MVNDO REGINA PRECAMINA FVNDO
AETERNAE PACIS ET PROPTER GAVDIA LVCIS

The head, hands and feet of Christ and the angel of St. Matthew are painted by another and Byzantine hand with brown flesh tint, while the flesh of the Imperial pair is whitish; they are also more thickly laid on so that small parts have fallen off. The ground is golden, the sky from bottom to top is green, pink and blue. It is a question whether those Byzantine parts were painted originally or whether they were transformed at a later period (XIVth century?) from the Echternach style into the more appreciated Byzantine manner. The latter seems more probable.

BIBLIOGRAPHY

ANTOLIN, *Cat. de los Códices latinos de la R. Biblioteca del Escorial,* IV, 280 ff.
BEISSEL, *Upsala,* p. 17.
BEISSEL, *Evang. Bch.,* p. 213, 220 f., 246, 333.
HASELOFF, *Egb. Psalter,* passim.
Museo Español, V, p. 503 ff.
SWARZENSKI, I, p. 93 note, 110 note, 113/115 note.
SWARZENSKI, II, p. 28 note 2, 34 f., 85 note 6.
VOEGE, p. 385.

photo Moreno, Madrid

58

MADRID, ESCORIAL. Cod. Aureus

SEE PLATE 57

FOL. 3: THE ENTHRONED VIRGIN WITH HENRY III (« HEINRICVS REX ») AND AGNES («AGNES REGINA »)

In the frame the four cardinal virtues. Inscription in frame:

O REGINA POLI ME REGEM SPERNERE NOLI
ME TIBI COMMENDO PRAESENTIA DONA FERENDO
PATREM CVM MATRE QVIN IVNCTAM PROLIS AMORE
VT SIS ADIVTRIX ET IN OMNI TEMPORE FAVTRIX

Over the architecture:

SPIRA FIT INSIGNIS HEINRICI MVNERE REGIS

The face (with the exception of the kerchief) and the hands of the Virgin are of the style of Byzantine painting (see pl. 57). The dress of the Virgin is blue, the cloak white, the drapery of Agnes is green, the cloak of Henry is pale pink, the tunic is tender yellow. This latter tint also predominates in the architecture and the throne. There is little light blue, green, pale pink, lilac and minium. The frame and medallions are golden, with pale pink stripes. There are details in gold. The ground is as in plate 57.

BIBLIOGRAPHY: *See plate 57.*

photo Moreno, Madrid

59

MADRID, ESCORIAL. Cod. Aureus

See plate 57

Fol. 133ᵛ: The Evangelist John

Bibliography: *See plate 57.*

photo Moreno, Madrid

60

MADRID, ESCORIAL. Cod. Aureus
See plate 57

Fol. 70ᵛ: Jesus helps his disciples in the storm (Matth. xvi, 24; Mark vi, 48).

BIBLIOGRAPHY: *See plate 57.*

photo Moreno, Madrid

61

MADRID, ESCORIAL. Cod. Aureus

See plate 57

Fol. 103: Raising of the youth at Nain

Bibliography: *See plate 57.*

photo Moreno, Madrid

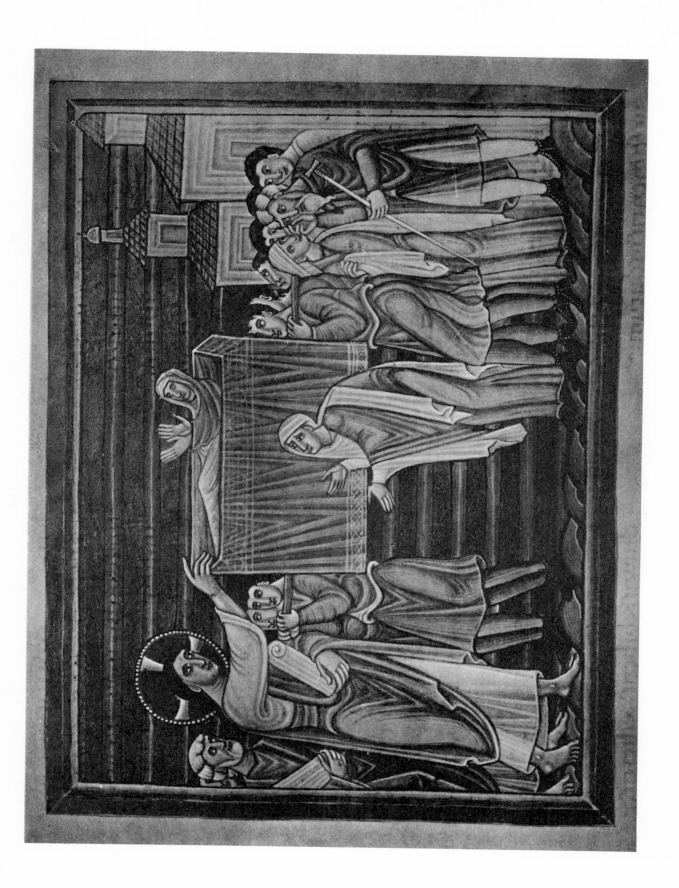

62

MADRID, ESCORIAL. Cod. Aureus

See plate 57

Fol. 109: Parable of the good Samaritan

Bibliography: *See plate 57.*

photo Moreno, Madrid

63

UPSALA, UNIVERSITY LIBRARY

GOSPELS (28 x 31,8 cm)

Written for the Cathedral of Goslar at the request of Henry III. Echternach.
Between 1050 (consecration of the Cathedral) and 1056 (death of Henry).

FOL. 3ᵛ: CHRIST CROWNS HENRY AND AGNES. IN THE FRAME THE SYM-
BOLS OF THE EVANGELISTS

Inscription at the top:

> PER ME REGNANTES VIVANT HEINRICVS ET AGNES

in the upper glory:

> CAELVM CAELI D(OMI)NO, TERRA(M) AVTE(M) DED(IT)

in the lower one:

> FILIIS HOMINV(M)

*The globe and mandorla are in gold with white inscriptions and diapered frame.
The ground exhibits changing colours. In the drapery the following tints chiefly
predominate: purple (the cloak of Christ, undergarments of the Imperial pair, in
a lighter tone in the cloak of Henry), white shaded with yellow, and blue (drapery
of Christ, paenula and kerchief of Agnes). The borders, crown, frame and grounds
of medallions are golden (cf. Beissel).*

BIBLIOGRAPHY

BEISSEL, *Upsala.*
SWARZENSKI, II, p. 28 note 2.

64

UPSALA, UNIVERSITY LIBRARY. Gospels of Henry III

See plate 63

Fol. 4: Henry presents the manuscript to Simon and Jude, the patron saints of the Cathedral of Goslar. In the frame are busts of angels

Inscription: heinricvs cesar svblimat moenia goslar. The year MXLV is a later addition.

The interior is in gold, the ground outside is coloured. The drapery of Henry and the cloak of Simon are purple. The undergarment of the latter is bluish white. Jude has an undergarment of shaded yellow and green and a blue cloak. The halo, medallions, bar of frame and borders are golden (cf. Beissel).

BIBLIOGRAPHY: *See plate 63.*

65

The Evangelist Luke

The ground is yellow, golden in the lunette. The undergarment is white with green lining and trimming; the cloak is purple blue, the curtains are green (cf. Beissel).

BIBLIOGRAPHY: *See plate 64.*

66

UPSALA, UNIVERSITY LIBRARY. Gospels of Henry III

See plate 63

THE EVANGELIST JOHN

The background is diaper-patterned, golden in the lunette. For the rest, purple (hangings of chair) and bright green (cloak of the Apostle and arm chair) are employed. The same tints are also used in the frame (cf. Beissel).

BIBLIOGRAPHY: *See plate 64.*

67

PARIS, BIBLIOTHÈQUE NATIONALE. Cod. lat. 9448
(16 x 32,6 cm)

ANTIPHONARY FROM PRÜM

Prüm, about 1000. Fol. 48 ff.: Colophon (according to Braun) by the hand of the scribe: Codicem istum cantus modulamine plenum, domni Hilde⸗ rici venerabilis abbatis tempore (d. 993) eiusque licentia Wickingi fidelis monachi impensis atque precatu scribere coeptum, domini vero Stephani (d. 1001) successoris prefati abbatis tempore atque benedictione diligentissime ut cernitur consummatum. Sancti Salvatoris domini nostri Jesu Christi al⸗ tari impositum. Huic sancto Prumiensi coenobio perhenni memoria no⸗ vimus traditum etc. (another doubtful inscription mentions on the contrary a monk Notker as the Scribe).

A. FOL. 28: PRESENTATION IN THE TEMPLE

B. FOL. 52ᵛ: DORMITION OF THE VIRGIN

In the miniatures of the Codex heavy dull colours are employed: chiefly sea green, slate blue, various tones of brown, and less frequently dirty yellow and brownish pink.

BIBLIOGRAPHY

BRAUN, p. 26, 45, 87 ff., ibid. further bibliography.
HASELOFF, *Egb. Psalter,* p. 91, 101, 103.
LABARTE, *Hist. d. Arts Industr. au Moyen Age, Album II,* pl. 90, Paris 1854.
SWARZENSKI, I, p. 116 note, 139 note, 141 note.
SWARZENSKI, II, p. 35 note 3, 42 note 4, 85 note 5, 87 notes 1⸗2, 114 note 1.

photo Prof. Haseloff, Kiel

68

PARIS, BIBLIOTHÈQUE NATIONALE. Cod. lat. 9448

See plate 67

A. Fol. 55ᵛ: The two Apostles and Simon Magus before Nero. Flight and Fall of Simon Magus

B. Fol. 56: The Martyrdom of St. Peter and St. Paul

Colours and Bibliography: *See plate 67.*

photo Prof. Haseloff, Kiel

69

MANCHESTER, RYLANDS LIBRARY. No. 7 (14,6 x 19,3 cm)

LECTIONARY

Prüm, eleventh century (between 1026 and 1068). COLOPHON: Virgo Maria Tuus Hunc Librum Dat Tibi Servus Abbas Ruopertus Prumiensis Nomine Dictus (1026⁄1068) etc.

FOL. 47: THE SYMBOL OF ST. MATTHEW

It imitates the symbol of the Carolingian Gospels in the Berlin Library, that were in Prüm.

The initial is in gold, the ground bright red, the bar of the frame is greenish. The figure is drawn in light violet brown ink (it is the diluted colour of the writing) and enriched by single broad lines in minium and gold. The halo is golden.

BIBLIOGRAPHY

HASELOFF, *Egb. Psalter*, p. 90 note 9, 101 note 2.
JAMES, p. 14 ff., plate 13⁄14.
MAX KEUFFER, *Das Prümer Lectionar ⁄ Trierisches Archiv I*, p. 3⁄17, 98.

N ILLO TEMPORE·
DIX IHS DISCIP SUS·
Scitis quia post biduum pascha fiet.
& filius hominis tradetur. ut crucifi
gatur." Tunc congregati sunt prīci
pes sacerdotum & seniores popli. in a
trium principis sacerdotum qui dice
batur caiphas." & consilium fecerunt

70

MANCHESTER, RYLANDS LIBRARY. No. 7

SEE PLATE 69

FOL. 45ᵛ-46: ENTRY INTO JERUSALEM

Drawing as plate 69. The background is sea green with white and red rosettes in dots.

BIBLIOGRAPHY: *See plate 69.*

71

SEE PLATE 69

FOL. 72ᵛ/73: THE MARIES AT THE TOMB

Drawing as in plate 69. The background at bottom is green, then light ochre (soil), then turquoise in two gradations, then again light ochre. The opening of the Sepulchre is brown purple. The shields are drawn with cinnabar.

BIBLIOGRAPHY: *See plate 69.*

72

MUNICH, STAATSBIBLIOTHEK. COD. LAT. 4456 (CIM. 60)
(24,1 x 29,7 cm)

SACRAMENTARY FROM THE CATHEDRAL TREASURY OF BAMBERG

According to the dedicatory verses (see below) it was made for King Henry the Second (1002-1014). The work of Ratisbon.

FOL. 11: THE CORONATION OF HENRY BY CHRIST

Saints Ulrich and Emmeram support the arms of the king who holds in his hands sword and lance handed to him by two angels. Inscription:

> ECCE CORONATVR DIVINITVS ATQVE BEATVR
> REX PIVS HEINRICVS PROAVORVM STIRPE POLOSVS
> HVIVS ŎDALRICVS COR REGIS SIGNET ET ACTVS
> EMMERAMMVS EI FAVEAT SOLAMINE DVLCI
> PROPVLSANS CVRAM SIBI CONFERT ANGELVS HASTAM
> APTAT ET HIC ENSEM CVI PROSIGNANDO TIMOREM

In the mandorla:

> CLEMENS XPE TVO LONGVM DA VIVERE XPICTO
> VT TIBI DEVOTVS NON PERDAT TEMPORIS VSVS

The intensity of the colours is very restrained. The tints of the background are alternately blue, olive, violet with small patterns in white and red. Henry wears a golden brown coat and a sapphire cloak. The drapery of Christ is blue working up to grey, the cloak is violet purple. The draperies of the two Saints and of the angels are green and brown purple, only the two albs are ochreous, almost orange coloured. There is much gold. The flesh-tint has a green ground colour and is modelled in an orange tint working up to white.

BIBLIOGRAPHY

BANGE, *Malerschule*, p. 31, 62 note, 64 note, 82, 103.
LEIDINGER, *Meisterwerke*, plates 12, 13.
SWARZENSKI, I, p. 63 ff. and passim, ibid. earlier bibliography.
SWARZENSKI, II, p. 34, 40 note 4, 46 note 2, 48.

photo Reusch, Munich

73

Fol. 11ᵛ: Miniature representing Henry with the provinces paying homage

Inscription:

ECCE TRIVMPHATIS TERRARVM PARTIBVS ORBIS
IN NVMERE GENTES DOMINANTIA IVSSA GERENTES
MVNERIBVS MVLTIS VENERANTVR CVLMEN HONORIS
TALIA NVNC GAVDE FIERI REX O BENEDICTE
NAM DITIONE TVA SVNT OMNIA IVRA SVBACTA
NEC MODO SVSCIPIAS CELI SVMTVRE CORONAS

The tunic of Henry is of an impure green with golden lights. The cloak is purple. The ornamented pieces on the shoulders and the knees are diapered. The armour-bearer is arrayed in a blue coat and red cloak. The provinces below have bright violet coats and green cloaks, those above have light and dark brown garments. The outlines are everywhere in a darker tone of the same tint, but never black. The flesh-tints are as in plate 72.

BIBLIOGRAPHY: *See plate 72.*

photo Reusch, Munich

74

MUNICH, STAATSBIBLIOTHEK. Cod. lat. 4456

See plate 72

FOL. 12: ST. GREGORY

The chasuble is blue; the flesh-tints as in plate 72, but the green tint is almost completely covered by the sorrel flesh-tone. The architecture is brownish purple and green, sometimes shaded in a darker tone of the same colour. The leaf ornaments in the frame are in minium, light green, violet, light blue, brownish purple, salmon-colour with yellow ground and relieved or rather outlined with white. The interior of the whole miniature is strewn over with a pattern of little white, red and green stars.

BIBLIOGRAPHY: *See plate 72.*

photo Reusch, Munich

75

MUNICH, STAATSBIBLIOTHEK. COD. LAT. 4456

SEE PLATE 72

FOL. 15: CRUCIFIX WITH THE VIRGIN AND ST. JOHN, SOL AND LUNA

In the corners of the frame are the symbols of the Evangelists. The plate is made by another and more occidental hand than plates 72-74. Inscription: « H CTAÖΦΡΩCIC ». (The apparent letter Φ is a mistaken borrowing from a Greek monogram of St. John standing under it). « Sancta Maria, Sanctus Iohannes ».

There is a purple ground. The tunic of the Virgin is auburn, the cloak is green with yellow, the kerchief blue and white. St. John wears a blue tunic and a cloak of a dull yellow colour. Sol is sorrel and Luna blue.

BIBLIOGRAPHY: *See plate 72.*

photo Reusch, Munich

76

MUNICH, STAATSBIBLIOTHEK. Cod. lat. 13601 (cim. 54)
(27,6 x 38,3 cm)

EVANGELISTARY

which, however, contains only the lessons for the church service and not in the order of the church year. Was executed at Ratisbon by order of the Abbess Uota of Niedermünster (1002/25).

FOL. 2: THE ABBESS UOTA HANDS OVER THE MS. TO THE VIRGIN. In the frame are the eight virtues. Inscriptions: In the medallion frame:

QVOD SEQVITVR PARTVM DE ME SCITOTE REMOTVM
HINC ERGO VIRGO DEVM GENVI PER PNEVMA SVPERNVM

In the segment above the Virgin: SANCTA MARIA (as monogram) DOMINA MVNDI ELECTA ⁄ VT SOL PVLCHRA VT LVNA... ⁄ ΘΗΕΟΘΟΚΟC (sic) ⁄ STELLA MARIS VIRGO VIRGINVM.

In the segment by the side of Uota: DOMINA VOTA (as monogram) AB⁄ BATISSA ⁄ VIRGO DEI GENETRIX DIVINO PIGNORE FELIX ⁄ SVSCIPE VOTA TVAE PROMTI SERVIMINIS V̊TAE.

In the outside border:

STEMMATA VIRTVTVM COMITANTIA LVMINE XPICTVM
COMPTA COROLLARIIS DANTVR PRO MVNERE IVSTIS.

Much gold is employed. The background is golden. The miniatures of the manu⁄ script display in the draperies light tints, particularly light blue, pink violet, green and yellow and also carmine. The leaf⁄work and architecture are violet pink, light blue and green. The frame is in gold. The inscriptions are gold on purple. The tendrils and animals are gold on a blue and green ground. The tints of the flesh are yellowish with white lights and drawn in red, green and a little black. The outside border with the inscription is dark brown and so is also the frame of the medallion and the ground of the two segments. In the draperies dark red and violet tints are employed; the Virgin wears a light green undergarment. The undergarment of the Christ child is light blue, the upper garment is in gold; those of the abbess are dark violet, sapphire (kerchief) and yellowish white.

BIBLIOGRAPHY

BANGE, *Malerschule*, passim. LEIDINGER, *Meisterwerke*, plates 14, 15. SWARZENSKI, I, p. 88 ff. and passim, ibid. further bibliography; II, passim.

photo Reusch, Munich

77

MUNICH, STAATSBIBLIOTHEK. Cod. lat. 13601
Evangelistary

See plate 76

A. Fol. 3ᵛ: Crucifix with Vita and Mors, Ecclesia and Synagoga

In the corners of the border Sol and Luna, the Resurrection of the Dead and the Rent Veil of the Temple. Inscription: In the frame of the upper Ellipse: ECCE CRVCIS HEREBUM COSMVM LOETVMQVE DIABLVM

HAEC PATRIS OMNIPOTENS VICIT SAPIENTA CHRISTVS

In the frame of the lower Ellipse:

SPIRAT POST DOMINVM SANCTORVM VITA PER AEVVM

MORS DEVICTA PERIS QVI CHRISTVM VINCERE GESTIS

On the ground beside Mors and Vita:

CRVX EST REPARATIO VITAE. CRVX EST DESTRVCTIO MORTIS

Under Ecclesia: PIA GRATIA SVRGIT IN ORTVM

Under Synagogue: LEX TENET OCCASVM

Under Sol: IGNEVS SOL OBSCVRATVR IN AETHERE QVIA SOL IVSTITIAE ⁄

PATITVR IN CRVCE

Under Luna:

ECLYPSIN PATITVR ET LVNA QVIA DE MORTE CHRISTI DOLET ECCLESIA

Under the resuscitated dead:

TERRA CONCVSSA MORTVOS REDDIDIT QVIA GENTILITAS CONVERSA ⁄

PER FIDEM VIVERE CEPIT

Under the curtain:

VELVM TEMPLI SCISSVM EST QUIA OBSCVRITAS LEGIS ABLATA EST

In the frame: MISTICA MORE CRVCIS FIT CONVERSATIO IVSTIS

LVX OPERVM LATVM TENET ET PERMANSIO LONGVM

CAELICA SPES TITVLVS SECRETA DEIQVE PROFVNDVM

Along the left side of the frame:

SCEMA CRVCIS TYPICVM MEDITATVR VITA BONORVM.

On the cross there are moral indications concerning its dimensions. On the ground near the crucifix are legends « which express the relation be⁄ tween Music, Grammar and Mathematics to the Divine rule » and give a graphic⁄schematic representation of the harmony of the spheres (see details in SWARZENSKI).

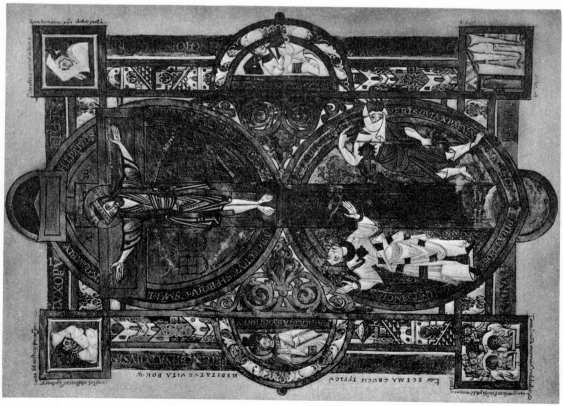

78

ROME, VATICANA. Ottob. Lat. 74 (22,5 x 27,8 cm)

Gospels of Henry II

Ratisbon, eleventh century (1014-24).

Fol. 193ᵛ: Emperor Henry II and above him the Dove of the Holy Ghost. To the left is Sapientia, to the right Prudentia, at the bottom is a scene of execution. In the corners are Iustitia, Pietas, Lex and Ius.

The framework, also in the medallions, is golden, and so is the ground behind the figures. The inscriptions are of gold on a blue background. The middle compartment is grained in blue and red with white dots. Henry wears a white undergarment, a blue coat, a violet cloak and a golden stole. The two half figures are in the same tints. For the rest the colours employed are blue and bluish tones, dark and light violet and white, only once a greenish tone and but little red (cf. Beissel).

BIBLIOGRAPHY

Bange, *Malerschule,* passim.
Beissel, *Vat. Min.,* p. 35 f., plate 18.
Swarzenski, I, p. 123 f.

79

BAMBERG, STAATSBIBLIOTHEK. Cod. Bibl. 95 (A. II. 46)
(17,6 x 24,5 cm)
Gospels

According to the dedicatory legend it was executed for a Heinricus rex pius.
To judge from the style Henry II must be meant. Abbey of Seeon. Between
1002 and 1014.

A. FOL. 7ᵛ: KING HENRY II

B. FOL. 8: VIRGIN

Inscription: HEINRICVS REX PIVS. SANCTA MARIA ΘEOTOCOS

*The interior of the arcade is golden, outside the ground is marbled. Only sea green
and light gradations or carmine working up to blue are employed. The tints of
the flesh of Henry are dark pink with darker shades relieved with white; in the
case of the Virgin it is sea green relieved with white. The lines of the features are
brown.*

BIBLIOGRAPHY

BANGE, *Malerschule*, p. 17 ff., 125 note.
FISCHER, *Katalog der Handschriften d. Kgl. Bibliothek zu Bamberg*, I, p. 3, 14 f.,
    ibid. further bibliography.
SWARZENSKI, I, p. 53 note, 64 note, 74 note, 79 note, 87 note, 110 note.
SWARZENSKI, II, p. 32, 37, 40 note 2, plates 26, 27.
VOEGE, p. 15 note 7.

80

COLOGNE, CATHEDRAL LIBRARY. Cod. 143 (19,5 x 29,5 cm)

Epistolary

It was executed at the command of Archbishop Everger of Cologne (985-99) probably for the Cologne Cathedral. School of Cologne.

Fol. 3ᵛ-4: The archbishop everger is in adoration before the Apostles Peter and Paul

Inscription: Left:

NEXVS ALME PATER VITIORVM SOLVE POTENTER
PAVLE DEO LECTVS PARITER TV SOLVE REATVS
CONSEQVOR VT VENIAM CHRISTO DONANTE SVPERNAM
EVERGERVS ARCHIEPISCOPVS

Right, in frame:

NOS VOCAT ESSE SVOS DEVOTA MENTE PATRONOS
PRESVL EVERGERVS CVIVS SVM NOMINE SCRIPTVS
ΑΓΙΟΣ ΠΗΤΡΟΣ ΗΓΙΟΣ ΠΑΥΛΥΣ

The colours are light blue and light pink without contours. In addition to these tints purple is employed. The background to the left contains green tints of various gradations at the bottom and purple at the top; to the right there is green at the bottom and light blue at the top. There is gold in the details of the costumes, haloes, legends and frame.

BIBLIOGRAPHY

Chroust, *Series* II, No. 7, plate 10, No. 8, plate 1.
Clemen, *Roman. Mon. Malerei*, p. 761.
Ehl, p. 48 ff., plates 14a and b; ibid. further bibliography.
Michel, I, 2, p. 728.

81

PARIS, BIBLIOTHÈQUE NATIONALE. Cod. lat. 817
(20 x 27 cm)

SACRAMENTARY

Coming from and executed for St. Gereon at Cologne. Cologne, end of the tenth century.

A. Fol. 15ᵛ: Maiestas Domini

Broken tints, considerably touched up with white. They are glaucous (globe), light blue (coat of Christ, wings of symbols), light yellow with brown (cloak of Christ), pale brown (spandrels). There are further employed green, a little red and gold (haloes, upper circle etc.). The mandorla is purple with golden stars.

B. Fol 59: Crucifix between the Virgin and St. John

The ground is purple, behind the Virgin and St. John it is of a lighter tint. The soil is tawny with golden flowers. The cross is golden. In the draperies the following tints are employed: greyish lilac (loin cloth), entirely broken into white (undergarment of the Virgin), blue (drapery of St. John) yellowish pink (cloak of St. John) deep green (cloak of Virgin) ⸱ cf. Ehl.

BIBLIOGRAPHY

Clemen, *Roman. Mon. Malerei*, p. 258 note 25, 760.
Ehl, p. 51 ff., plates 15⸱23, ibid. further bibliography.
Leroquais, p. 97 ff., plates 17⸱19.
Michel, I, 2, p. 728.
Schramm, p. 78.
Swarzenski, I, p. 119 note, 120 note.

photo Prof. Haseloff, Kiel

82

COLOGNE, STADTARCHIV. Cod. 312
(24,1 x 32,7 cm)
Gospels from St. Gereon in Cologne

Cologne, beginning of the eleventh century.

A. Fol. 21: The Evangelist Matthew

The ground is dirty green and purple brown relieved with white. The coat is blue, the cloak is violet brown, both touched up with white. The halo is golden, throne in gold with white tendrils and red cushions, the frame is blue between gold edges.

B. Fol. 160: The Evangelist John

The colours are yellow and pink. The foreground is green, the cloak violet, the earth knolls are dark green, the halo and book scroll are in gold (cf. Ehl).

BIBLIOGRAPHY

Clemen, *Roman. Mon. Malerei*, p. 258 note 25, 760.
Ehl, p. 79 ff., plates 25/27, ibid. further bibliography.
Michel, I, 2, p. 729.

photo Prof. Haseloff, Kiel

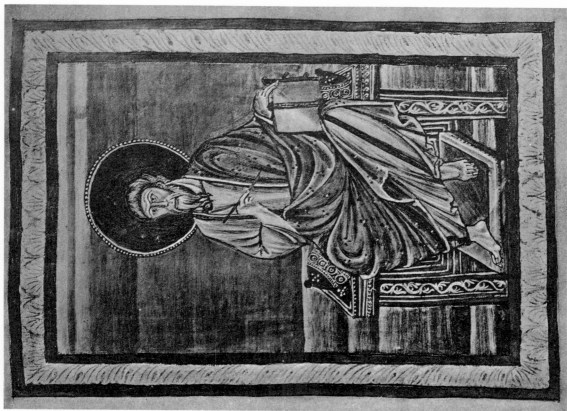

83

MILAN, AMBROSIANA. c. 53 sup.
GOSPELS

Cologne, first half of the eleventh century.

A. FOL. 118: THE EVANGELIST LUKE

The background is in stripes varying from dark green to violet. The tunic is blue, the cloak is yellow, the throne golden.

B. FOL. 19: THE EVANGELIST MATTHEW

The tunic is light grey, the cloak in a tone between pink and violet.

BIBLIOGRAPHY

EHL, p. 103 ff., plates 38-41.
MICHEL I, 2, p. 729.
MUÑOZ, *Miniature della Scuola di Colonia - L'Arte* XI, fasc. III (reprod.).

photo Prof. Haseloff, Kiel

84

A. MILAN, AMBROSIANA. C. 53 SUP.

SEE PLATE 83

FOL. 3ᵛ: ST. JEROME OFFERS A SCROLL TO A DEACON

The ground is violet, green and pink, touched up with white. The undergarment of St. Jerome is pink, shaded in yellow. The paenula is light violet. The throne is pink with golden steps. The haloes and footstools are in gold, the frame is violet and grey between golden bars.

BIBLIOGRAPHY: *See plate 83.*

B. GIESSEN, UNIVERSITÄTSBIBLIOTHEK. COD. 660
(21,2 x 26,3 cm)

GOSPELS

Cologne, first half of the eleventh century.

FOL. 2ᵛ: ST. JEROME WITH HIS SCRIBE

The ground is purple brown, red, yellow, with white separating lines. The undergarment is in a tint between grey and blue, the chasuble is rock lilac, merging into grey. The throne is in a heavy sea green tint, the drapery of the scribe is in a dirty blue tint with reddish lights (cf. Ehl).

BIBLIOGRAPHY

EHL, p. 105 ff., plates 42-45.

photo Prof. Haseloff, Kiel

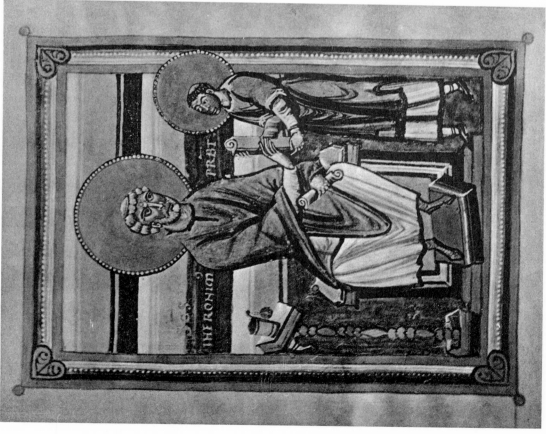

85

GIESSEN, UNIVERSITÄTSBIBLIOTHEK. Cod. 660

See plate 84 b

Fol. 188: Crucifixion (At the beginning of the Gospels of St. John).

Uncoloured background. The soil is blue with golden flowers. The cross and frame are golden. The loin cloth is greyish violet. The tints of the flesh have bluish shades.

Bibliography: *See plate 84 b.*

photo Prof. Haseloff, Kiel

86

DARMSTADT, LANDESBIBLIOTHEK. Cod. 1640 (22 x 29 cm)

GOSPELS OF THE ABBESS HITDA OF MESCHEDE (WESTPHALIA)

Dedicatory legend:

HVNC LIBRVM SANCTAE WALBVRGAE HITDA ABBATISSA PRO SE SVISQVE

Cologne, first half of the eleventh century. The codex contains in addition an inventory of the objects which the Abbess Hitda presented to the abbey.

A. FOL. 172: THE EVANGELIST JOHN

The ground is sea green, grey and yellow with white flowers. The drapery is pink, the cloak is pale yellow, the halo and borders golden. The general tone is light.

B. FOL. 78: THE EVANGELIST MARK

The ground is in reddish, brown and blue tints. The undergarment is blue, the cloak is pale yellow, the throne brown, the footstool blue (cf. Ehl).

BIBLIOGRAPHY

CLEMEN, *Roman. Mon. Malerei,* p. 131, 258 note 25, 760.
CHROUST, *Series* II, N. 23, pl. 10; ibid. further bibliography.
EHL, p. 108 ff., reproductions 46⁄50, 52⁄56, ibid. further bibliography.
A. LUDORFF, *Die Bau⁄ u. Kunstdenkm. v. Westfalen, Kreis Meschede,* p. 59, ibid. reproductions of all the miniatures.
MICHEL, I, 2, p. 729.
SWARZENSKI, I, p. 119 note, 143.
SWARZENSKI, II, p. 35 note 8, 86 note 8.

87

DARMSTADT, LANDESBIBLIOTHEK. Cod. 1640

See plate 86

A. FOL. 117: STORM ON THE SEA

The background is blue with a pinkish grey tone; the ship is yellow with grey and black tones; the sail is brown with a good deal of white. The haloes are golden.

B. FOL. 75: THE BAPTISM OF CHRIST

A great deal of blue with white (water), brown and white (river god, St. John, section of sky). There is gold in the haloes and plants (cf. EHL).

BIBLIOGRAPHY: *See plate 86.*

photo Provinzial-Denkmal-Archiv, Münster

88

STUTTGART, LANDESBIBLIOTHEK. Cod. bibl. 402
Gospels of Gundold
See plate 89

Cologne, second quarter of the eleventh century.

Fol. 9ᵛ: The Crucifixion with the Virgin, St. John and the founder (13 x 18 cm).

Inscription: MP ΘΥ S̄ IOHANNES

The background from bottom to top dirty green, minium, sea green working up to light green; the Virgin is in a sorrel tunic and white kerchief, St. John wears a brown tunic and a bluish violet cloak. The tints of the flesh are pink with darker shades and a black violet drawing. There are erasures round the head of the founder and on St. John and the Virgin.

BIBLIOGRAPHY

Bange, *Abdinghof,* p. 98.
Clemen, *Roman. Mon. Malerei,* p. 258 note 25.
Ehl, p. 143, reprod. 57-59.
Swarzenski, I, p. 91 note.

photo Prof. Haseloff, Kiel

89

Fol. 10: Maiestas Domini with the symbols of the Evangelists
and the four major Prophets

Underneath the picture: ΓΥΝΔΩΛΔΥC

*The general tone is bluish violet, with the exception of the cross of the halo, which
is ochre-coloured, and the book. The background in shaded stripes of violet,
bluish grey and violet. The cloak of Christ is yellow, the tunic ochre-coloured.
The Greek inscription is green.*

BIBLIOGRAPHY: *See plate 88.*

photo Prof. Haseloff, Kiel

90

A. STUTTGART, LANDESBIBLIOTHEK. COD. BIBL. 402

SEE PLATE 88

FOL. 71ᵛ: THE EVANGELIST JOHN

The background from bottom to top is pink, green merging into yellow, blue working up to violet, covered with thinly painted plants. The tunic is light green, the cloak is purple with gold strokes. The tints of the flesh are dark brown.

BIBLIOGRAPHY: *See plate 88.*

photo Prof. Haseloff, Kiel

B. DARMSTADT, LANDESMUSEUM. A. E. 679 (15 x 18 cm)

GOSPELS FROM ST. ANDREAS AT COLOGNE
AND WRITTEN FOR ST. ANDREAS

Cologne, first half of the eleventh century.

FOL. 82: THE EVANGELIST MARK

The drapery is pale blue, the cloak violet.

BIBLIOGRAPHY

EHL, p. 100 ff., reprod. 35.

photo Rheinisches Museum, Cologne

91

COLOGNE, PRIESTERSEMINAR. Cod. 753 b

GOSPELS FROM STA. MARIA AD GRADUS IN COLOGNE

Cologne, second quarter of the eleventh century.

FOL. 1ᵛ: MAIESTAS DOMINI WITH THE SYMBOLS OF THE EVANGELISTS AND THE FOUR MAJOR PROPHETS

The ground is golden with sorrel traverses; the interior of the large circle is blue with golden stars, the margins are glaucous and sorrel with white. The tunic is pale blue working up to grey, the cloak is yellow with brown. The draperies of the prophets are greyish white, dark brown, red and green. The haloes are golden; the scrolls are ochreous with sorrel shades (cf. Ehl).

BIBLIOGRAPHY

EHL, p. 158 ff., reproductions 62/65; ibid. further bibliography.
SWARZENSKI, I, p. 100 note.

photo Prof. Haseloff, Kiel

92

BAMBERG, STAATSBIBLIOTHEK. Cod. bibl. 94 (A. II. 18)
(18,9 x 24,4 cm)
Gospels

Cologne, second quarter of the eleventh century.

A. Fol. 9ᵛ: Maiestas Domini with the symbols of the Evangelists and the four major Prophets

Very strong and pure colours, no contours. The ground is golden. The cloak of Christ is in ochre, the tunic is white with blue shades. The upper halo is purple, the lower blue, both adorned with golden stars. The earth globe is cinnabar inside, green outside. The same tints are also employed in the half figures. The flesh-tint consists of various tones artistically composed (brown, cinnabar, violet and green).

B. Fol. 154ᵛ: Christ as redeemer of the world

In the globe are the four elements, angels holding the footstool for Christ, and scenes of baptism. Legend of the traverse of the globe. Inscription:

OMNIA PER CHRISTVM FACTA SVNT ET SINE CHRISTO FACTVM EST NIHIL

The colours resemble those of A.

BIBLIOGRAPHY

Clemen, *Roman. Mon. Malerei,* p. 131, 258 note 25, 304.
Ehl, p. 171 ff., reprod. 69-74, 113; ibid. further bibliography.
Michel, I, 2, p. 730.

93

BAMBERG, STAATSBIBLIOTHEK. Cod. bibl. 94 (A. II. 18)
See plate 92

A. Fol. 16: The Evangelist Matthew

Golden ground. The wings of the angel are composed of violet, yellow, green and blue. The tunic is blue, the cloak brown purple.

B. Fol. 156: The Evangelist John

The cloak is yellow, the drapery violet, the throne a dirty pea green, the book is carmine (cf. Ehl).

Bibliography: *See plate 92.*

94

STUTTGART, LANDESBIBLIOTHEK. COD. BIBL. FOL. 21
(22 x 29 cm)

GOSPELS FROM ST. GEREON IN COLOGNE

Contains entries referring to consecrations of St. Gereon from the years 1067, 1068 and 1069. Cologne, the forties of the eleventh century.

A. FOL. 67: THE EVANGELIST MARK

The background from bottom to top is chrome yellow, sap green and minium. The cloak is light violet with golden ornaments. The undergarment is pale blue. The seat is brown, the cushion carmine. The halo is golden.

B. FOL. 19: THE EVANGELIST MATTHEW

The background is minium, chrome yellow and turquoise. The tunic is pale blue the cloak and throne purple violet. The scroll is uncoloured. The halo is golden. The tints of the flesh are whitish pink, relieved with white.

BIBLIOGRAPHY

BANGE, *Abdinghof,* p. 97.
CHROUST, *Series* II, N. 8, plate 4.
CLEMEN, *Roman. Mon. Malerei,* p. 137.
EHL, p. 193 ff., reproductions 79–81.
MICHEL, I, 2, p. 730.

photo Rheinisches Museum, Cologne

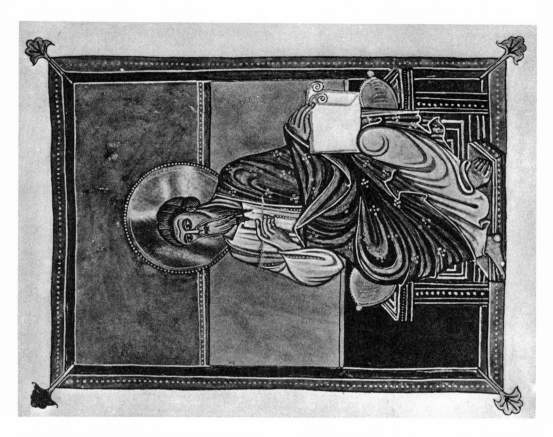

95

BERLIN, KUPFERSTICHKABINETT DER STAATL. MUSEEN
Ms. 78 A 3 (16 x 31 cm)

GOSPELS FROM THE ABBEY OF ABDINGHOF NEAR PADERBORN

Preserved in 1270 in the abbey of SS Peter and Paul at Paderborn. Cologne, about 1060.

FOL. 1ᵛ⁄2: MISSION OF CHRIST TO THE APOSTLES (Mark XVI, 15).

Gold ground. The draperies are greenish, light blue, lilac brown, brownish violet, all shaded in a darker tone and relieved with a great deal of white. The tints of the flesh are white with violet and minium working up to yellow in the shades. The drawing of the features is brown and black. The hair is lightly glaucous or greyish lilac working up to a brownish tint. The frame outside is lilac, inside of a brownish violet tint.

BIBLIOGRAPHY

BANGE, *Abdinghof*, ibid. further bibliographical references and repr.
EHL, p. 203 ff., reproductions 82⁄87, 115, 116, ibid. further bibliography.

96

A. BERLIN, KUPFERSTICHKABINETT. Ms. 78 A 3

SEE PLATE 95

FOL. 13^v: MAIESTAS DOMINI

The mandorla from the interior towards the outside is grey, sapphire and golden. The ground is for the rest grey on the top, and brownish lilac at the bottom; to the right in between are narrow stripes in minium, gold and grey. The drapery of Christ is greenish grey, the cloak is of a dull light brown with minium lining. The rainbow is light green, the halo in silver and gold. The animals are painted in various tones of brown, the wings are light brown working up to reddish and sapphire tints. The draperies of the angel are heavy sea green and lilac with pale yellow minium lining. The tints of the flesh as in plate 95.

BIBLIOGRAPHY: *See plate 95.*

B. FREIBURG (BADEN), UNIVERSITÄTSBIBLIOTHEK
Ms. 360a (22 x 30 cm)

SACRAMENTARY

Cologne, about 1060.

FOL. 15^v: CRUCIFIX

Purple ground. The cross and halo are in silver, the last with golden cross, and both with red, white and black dotted contours. The apron is lilac. The board for the inscription is white lilac and blue with red drawing. The suppedaneum is red with white, and blue with red drawing. The tints of the flesh are reddish with white lights and sorrel drawing. The hair is blue with red strokes (cf. Braun).

BIBLIOGRAPHY

BANGE, *Abdinghof*, p. 101, ibid. further bibliography.
BRAUN, p. 8 ff. with 2 plates.
EHL, p. 210 ff., reproduction 88.

97

MUNICH, STAATSBIBLIOTHEK. Cod. lat. 9475 (cim. 142)
(17 x 23 cm)
Gospels

Bremen? Saint Willehad is distinguished by a vigil. First half of the eleventh century.

A. FOL. 15^v: THE EVANGELIST MATTHEW. Beside the symbol there is the dove of the Holy Ghost.

Purple ground. The tunic is sea green with minium hem, the cloak is entirely light greyish violet. The haloes are in minium. There are mostly black folds. Before each Apostle there is a page with purple textile pattern.

B. FOL. 174^v: THE EVANGELIST JOHN. Beside the symbol there is the dove of the Holy Ghost.

Purple ground. The tunic is light violet; the cloak is tawny, the throne and halo are in minium. There is no gold. The pictures, the general tone of which is red and purple, produce the impression of uniformity of colour.

BIBLIOGRAPHY

BANGE, *frühroman. Hss.*, p. 1, 7.
DOERING and VOSS, p. 91.
B. RIEHL, *Zur bayer. Kunstgesch.*, I, p. 31.
SWARZENSKI, I, p. 16 note 13, 86 note.

photo Reusch, Munich

98

MANCHESTER, RYLANDS LIBRARY
Cod. No. 87 (Haigh Hall 17) (19,2 x 24,2 cm)
EVANGELIARY

Bremen? about 1000. The entry of the XVII/XVIII century runs as follows:

HOC EVANGELIORVM CODICE VSVS FVIT S. ANSCHARIVS DVM
ESSET IN VIVIS, ET MVLTIS DEINDE SAECVLIS IN ECCLESIA
BREMENSI VELVTI SACER ADSERVATVS EST

A. FOL. 64: THE EVANGELIST ST. MARK. Beside the symbol there is the dove of the Holy Ghost.

The ground is purple with white tendrils, the undergarment is blue, the cloak is yellow the dove is white, the clouds are blue.

B. FOL. 158ᵛ: THE SYMBOL OF ST. JOHN

The square is purple, the medallion orange-coloured with blue palmette frame. The eagle is saturnine red with vermilion and brown drawing. The book is blue, the halo is golden.

BIBLIOGRAPHY

DOERING and VOSS, p. 90 f.
JAMES, p. 157 ff.
SWARZENSKI, I, p. 86 note.

99

HILDESHEIM, CATHEDRAL TREASURY. No. 18 (20 x 27 cm)

GOSPELS WRITTEN AT THE REQUEST OF BISHOP
BERNWARD OF HILDESHEIM (985⁄1022)

Hildesheim, beginning of the eleventh century. Dedicatory inscription:

HVNC EGO BERNWARDVS CODICEM CONSCRIBERE FECI
ATQVE MEAS, VT CERNIS, OPES SVPERADDERE JVBENS
DILECTO DOMINI DEDERAM SANCTO MICHAHELI
SIT ANATHEMA DEI, QVISQVIS SIBI DEMPSERIT ILLVM

FOL. 76: THE EVANGELIST MARK

The background is green on the top and light blue with red strokes at the bottom; the cloak is red, the undergarment white. The architecture is in purple, black and white, gold and a little yellow. The medallion and the halo of the Apostle are in gold (cf. Josten).

BIBLIOGRAPHY

BANGE, *frühroman. Hss.*, p. 4 ff.
BEISSEL, *Bernward Evang.*, reproduction.
DOERING and VOSS, p. 90.
HASELOFF, *Egb. Psalter*, p. 126 ff.
JOSTEN.
SWARZENSKI, I, p. 84 f., 89 note.

100

SEE PLATE 99

FOL. 175ᵛ: THE EVANGELIST JOHN AND THE ASCENSION OF CHRIST

The ground above is light grey, below it is purple with blue ornament. Christ is in white, the section of the sky is gold with grey clouds. The throne and cloak of St. John are red. The undergarment is white. The top of the table to the left is yellow. There is much gold (cf. Josten).

BIBLIOGRAPHY: *See plate 99.*

photo Renger-Patzsch, Bad Harzburg

101

HILDESHEIM, CATHEDRAL TREASURY. No. 18
SEE PLATE 99

A. FOL. 119: Q(UONIAM QUIDEM)

Golden forms. The interior background of the initials is chiefly green and blue, but contains also purple and lilac with numerous white dots. The ornament in the body of the initials is in light and dark purple. Outside the letters is a purple ground.

B. FOL. 179: IN (PRINCIPIO ERAT)

The colours are as in A.

BIBLIOGRAPHY: *See plate 99.*

photo Renger-Patzsch, Bad Harzburg

102

HILDESHEIM, CATHEDRAL TREASURY. No. 61
(34,5 x 45,3 cm)
BIBLE OF ST. BERNWARD

Hildesheim, beginning of the eleventh century. In its style it is related to plate 107.

FOL. 1: TITLE MINIATURE WITH MOSES (after the beginning of Genesis which is inscribed on the book which he holds) AND ECCLESIA(?) BY THE SIDE OF THE CROSS

The ground is patterned in two tones of purple; behind the tendril work it is blue and lilac with light dots and behind the figures it is golden. The cross is in gold. The alb of Moses is white with brown, the chasuble is violet, the halo is blue. The garment of Ecclesia (?) is light green with white and violet. The halo is green. The curtain is white with green and blue (cf. Beissel).

BIBLIOGRAPHY

BEISSEL, *St. Bernward,* p. 24 f.
BANGE, *frühroman. Hss.,* p. 11 ff.
DOERING and VOSS, p. 90.
JOSTEN, p. 83.
SWARZENSKI, I, p. 84 f.

photo Renger-Patzsch, Bad Harzburg

103

HILDESHEIM, CATHEDRAL TREASURY. No. 33
(23,5 x 29,2 cm)

GOSPELS, WRITTEN IN 1011 BY GUNTBALD AT THE REQUEST OF
ST. BERNWARD

Dedicatory inscription:

ANNO HEROICAE NATIVITATIS MILLESIMO VNDECIMO, INDICT IX, DO-
MINO S(E)C(VN)DO HEINRICO SCEPTRIS REGNI PRAEFVLGENTE, BERN-
WARDO QVOQ(VE) VENERABILI HILDESHEMENSIS ECCL(ESI)AE IVRE
PONTIFICALI PRAESIDENTE GVNTBALDVS, INDIGNVS ET PECCATOR,
DIACONVS, HVNC LIBRVM IV EVANGELIORVM P(RAE)NOMINATO PONTI-
FICI DEI CONSVMMAVIT.

On fol. 270 there is besides the same dedicatory inscription as in plate 99.
Hildesheim. 1011.

FOL. 204ᵛ: THE EVANGELIST MATTHEW

BIBLIOGRAPHY

BEISSEL, *St. Bernward*, p. 24.
BANGE, *frühroman. Hss.*, p. 11ff.
HASELOFF, *Egb. Psalter*, p. 126 ff.
JOSTEN, p. 82 ff.
SWARZENSKI, I, p. 84 ff.

photo Renger-Patzsch, Bad Harzburg

104

HILDESHEIM, CATHEDRAL TREASURY. No. 19
(25 x 32 cm)
SACRAMENTARY OF GUNTBALD

Hildesheim 1014. Dedicatory verse (fol. 3ᵛ):

CONTVLIT HVNC LIBRVM DIVINIS VSIBVS APTVM
PRESVL BERNWARDVS VIRTVTEM STEMMATE FVLTVS
ECCLESIAE AD GAZAS MICHAHELIS IN ORDINE SVMMI ETC.

By a later hand but prior to the twelfth century are added the following lines (fol. 243): ANNO DOMINICE INCARNATIONIS MXIIII SUB BERNWARDO PONTIFICE GVNTPOLDVS DIACONVS HVIVS LIBRI SCRIPTOR CLARVIT

FOL. 4ᵛ: INITIAL T(E IGITUR) WITH CRUCIFIX, THE VIRGIN AND ST. JOHN

The background consists of wide stripes of lighter and darker purple, separated by blue and lilac bands. The initials are in gold and silver on grounds dotted in blue and greenish white. The haloes are in gold. The frame is purple between gold and silver bars.

BIBLIOGRAPHY

BANGE, *frühroman. Hss.*, p. 11 ff.
JOSTEN, p. 82 f.
BEISSEL, *St. Bernward*, p. 26; ibid. further bibliography.

photo Renger-Patzsch, Bad Harzburg

105

HILDESHEIM, CATHEDRAL TREASURY. No. 34
(23,5 x 30,5 cm)

GOSPELS

Attributed to bishop Hezilo of Hildesheim (1054/79), but probably of the first half of the eleventh century. Hildesheim.

FOL. 163ᵛ: THE EVANGELIST JOHN

BIBLIOGRAPHY

BANGE, *frühroman. Hss.,* p. 14 f.
BEISSEL, *Evang. Bch.,* p. 289, 334.
DOERING and VOSS, p. 90.
JOSTEN, p. 88, Plate 1/4.

photo Renger-Patzsch, Bad Harzburg

106

GÖTTINGEN, UNIVERSITÄTSBIBLIOTHEK
COD. THEOL. FOL. 231 (27 x 34 cm)
SACRAMENTARY FROM FULDA

Fulda, ca. 975.

FOL. 60: ON TOP THE CRUCIFIXION WITH THE THIEVES, STEPHATON AND
LONGINUS, SOL AND LUNA, THE RESURRECTED DEAD. AT THE BOTTOM
CHRIST BEFORE PILATE

*The soil is yellow, the sky of a light tint, chiefly lilac. The draperies are chiefly
of sea green, dark violet, and brick red tints (cf. Zimmermann, p. 10).*

BIBLIOGRAPHY

RICHTER-SCHÖNFELDER, reproduction.
ZIMMERMANN, *Fulda*, p. 2 ff.

107

BERLIN, STAATSBIBLIOTHEK. THEOL. LAT. FOL. 192
(20,8 x 28,5 cm)

FRAGMENT OF SACRAMENTARY

Fulda, towards 975.

The front cover of binding contains a calendar picture. Annus with the four seasons, the busts of Day and Night and the pictures of the Months.

Very subdued in colour: brownish purple, dark green and greyish blue predominate. There is also gold, some dull yellow and very little thin minium and light blue.

BIBLIOGRAPHY

HASELOFF, *Malerschule,* p. 74; ibid. further bibliographical references.
ZIMMERMANN, *Fulda,* p. 39, 50 ff.

108

BAMBERG, STAATSBIBLIOTHEK. Cod. lit. 1 (A. II. 52)
(16,5 x 22,4 cm)
Sacramentary from Fulda

Perhaps a gift of Henry II or of the abbey of Fulda to Bamberg. On the cover a Byzantine ivory Madonna in half figure. Fulda, tenth or eleventh century, certainly after 993, probably executed during the period of the abbacy of Erkanbald of Fulda (997-1011).

A. Fol. 25: Annunciation to the Shepherds and Birth of Christ

The architecture is irregularly gilded with large brush-strokes. The background of the Annunciation from bottom to top is blue, turquoise blue, and violet. The same colours are also employed in the birth of Christ.

B. Fol. 126^v: St. Bonifacius baptizes and is killed

The draperies are green, blue, carmine and Naples yellow. The soil at the top is greenish yellow, at the bottom blue. The sky is blue at the top and green at the bottom. There is a great deal of drawing and outlining in black (evidently with the brush).

BIBLIOGRAPHY

Richter-Schönfelder, p. xi f.
Zimmermann, *Fulda,* p. 21 ff., ibid. further bibliography.

109

BAMBERG, STAATSBIBLIOTHEK, Cod. lit. 1 (A. II. 52)

SEE PLATE 108

A. FOL. 170: ST. MARTIN DIVIDES HIS CLOAK

The soil is green, the sky is blue. Otherwise the colours employed are yellowish pink working up to scarlet and a little green. Frequently there are uncoloured spaces.

B. FOL. 144: THE MARTYRDOM OF ST. LAWRENCE

Colours as in A.

BIBLIOGRAPHY: *See plate* 108.

IIO

ROME, VATICANA. Cod. Vat. lat. 3548 (20 x 28,5 cm)

Sacramentary from Fulda

Fulda, second quarter of eleventh century. According to an entry of the eleventh century (fol. 3ᵛ) prior to 1054.

A. Fol. 8: Birth of Christ and Annunciation to the shepherds

The soil is pale green with violet strokes. The sky is blue. The couch is light sea green. The pillow is white with violet shades. The manger is light yellow with light violet shades. In the drapery there are many violet and sea green shades. The flesh-tints whitish with tawny shades, that of Joseph is darker. The outlines are violet.

B. Fol. 14: Adoration of the Magi

The background is saturnine red, otherwise as in A.

BIBLIOGRAPHY

Richter-Schönfelder, p. XII., ibid. further bibliography.
Zimmermann, *Fulda,* p. 29 ff.

III

MUNICH, STAATSBIBLIOTHEK. Cod. lat. 10077 (cim. 173)
(17,5 x 25,5 cm)

Sacramentary from the Cathedral treasury of Verdun

The saints fix Corvey as the place of provenance; the calendar was arranged for Verdun in the eleventh century. The cover contains ivory reliefs (cf. Goldschmidt I, No. 67). Fulda or Corvey? latter half of the tenth century.

Fol. 12: Crucifixion with the Virgin and St. John and worshipping ecclesiastic

The outside borders are (going from without) golden, violet and green. The beams of the cross are golden with blue edge. The drapery of Christ is violet, the flesh-tint is pink and white. The background inside the space behind the horizontal beams of the cross is left uncoloured (the legend is gold). The slanting legends in the background are white. In the ornaments the following tints are employed: gold, light pink and minium and blue. A green tint is used only in the frames and medallions. (cf. Vol. 1, plate 83 B).

BIBLIOGRAPHY

Lehmann, *Corveyer Studien - Abhdlg. d. Bayr. Akad. d. Wiss., phil-hist. Kl. XXX, 5. Abh.,* p. 40 ff.
Zimmermann, *Fulda,* p. 35 ff.

photo Reusch, Munich

112

LUCCA, BIBLIOTECA PUBBLICA. Cod. 1275 (Lucchesini 5)
FRAGMENTS OF A SACRAMENTARY

Mainz? (the saints point to the district of Mainz), tenth or eleventh century.

A. FOL. 21ᵛ: THE MARTYRDOM OF ST. LAWRENCE

Colours: The background is green, at the top it is black with golden stars. The draperies of the king are blue and red. The idol and its pedestal are in gold.

B. FOL. 12: THE ASCENSION

Very light colours. The draperies of Christ are white, those of the angels are red-dish white. The earth hillocks are green, red and blue. The background is striped (from bottom to top) in green, red, blue and white (cf. Ebner).

BIBLIOGRAPHY

BEISSEL, *Zeitschrift für Christl. Kunst*, VII, p. 79.
EBNER, *Missale*, p. 66 ff.
RICHTER-SCHÖNFELDER, p. XIV.
ZIMMERMANN, *Fulda*, p. 102, ibid. earlier bibliography.

photo Prof. Haseloff, Kiel